D1017279

WORLD'S BEST COIN TRICKS

BOB LONGE

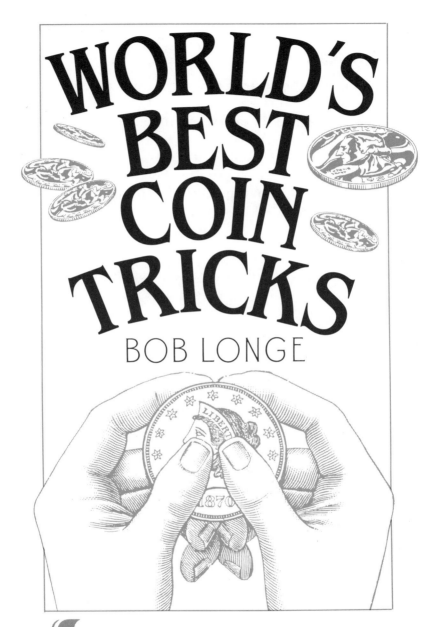

Sterling Publishing Co., Inc.   New York

Dedication

Anyone who performs coin tricks owes a debt of gratitude to two masters of manipulation. Many of the tricks presented here were invented or improved by them.

J.B. Bobo is probably the father of modern coin magic, and one of the great teachers of magic.

Milton Kort is an ingenious, brilliant innovator, and the most skillful close-up performer I have ever seen.

Library of Congress Cataloging-in-Publication Data

Longe, Bob, 1928–
    World's best coin tricks / by Bob Longe.
        p.   cm.
    Includes index.
    Summary: Includes instructions for performing more than fifty tricks, with varying degrees of difficulty, using ordinary coins.
    ISBN 0-8069-8660-3
    1. Coin tricks—Juvenile literature. [1. Coin tricks. 2. Magic tricks.] I. Title.
GV1559.L66 1992
793.8—dc20   92-11370
                                    CIP
                                     AC

10 9 8 7 6 5 4 3 2

First paperback edition published in 1993 by
Sterling Publishing Company, Inc.
387 Park Avenue South, New York, N.Y. 10016
© 1992 by Bob Longe
Distributed in Canada by Sterling Publishing
% Canadian Manda Group, P.O. Box 920, Station U
Toronto, Ontario, Canada M8Z 5P9
Distributed in Great Britain and Europe by Cassell PLC
Villiers House, 41/47 Strand, London WC2N 5JE, England
Distributed in Australia by Capricorn Link Ltd.
P.O. Box 665, Lane Cove, NSW 2066
Manufactured in the United States of America
All rights reserved

Sterling ISBN 0-8069-8660-3 Trade
           0-8069-8661-1 Paper

CONTENTS

INTRODUCTION

Are you ready to perform miracles? With the aid of this book, you can do so with coins. The sleights are easily learned and the tricks are astonishing. Unique in a collection of coin tricks is the inclusion of fourteen tricks requiring no sleight of hand whatever.

"The hand is quicker than the eye." Old-time carnival performers would bark out this line as part of their patter, and it became perhaps the best-known line in magic. Unfortunately, this has led many aspiring magicians to believe that incredible speed and skill were essential to performing sleight-of-hand tricks. With the vast majority of sleights, this is *absolutely untrue*. As you will see, you don't have to be fast, but you *must* be smooth and natural.

Does this call for countless hours of dull, repetitious practice? Certainly you must practise, but work a few minutes a day on each sleight and, before you know it, you'll have attained mastery. The few tricks that require considerable practice will reward you beyond the effort expended.

Some magicians perform coin sleights, but they never do coin *tricks*. This is fine if you just want to demonstrate how clever you are, but it's not necessarily entertaining. Let's take an elementary example. The magician places a coin in his left hand, and then shows that the hand is empty. He opens the right hand, and there's the coin. He didn't *really* put it in the left hand. This is *not* magic.

Let's try it this way: The magician places a coin in his left hand and promptly smacks the coin against the top of his head. He coughs, covering his mouth with his right hand, and, sure enough, he's coughed out the coin. It has passed right through his empty head. Now *this* is magic. Not great magic, but a perfect warm-up.

A coin disappears from one hand. The most obtuse member of the audience will eventually figure out that it's in the other hand. A coin disappears, so it should reappear *somewhere*. The trick is complete. Or, if the coin doesn't reappear, you should be able to show that both hands are empty. That, too, is magic. The point: Don't do sleights, do magic.

This book will teach you most of the best coin tricks ever invented, along with the easiest ways to accomplish them. I don't use trick coins, boxes which cause coins to disappear, or anything requiring special equipment or preparation. If you really are "magic," you should be able to perform your miracles at any time, with any coins. Every trick here can be done with borrowed coins; in fact, I recommend their use whenever possible.

Here you're given excellent coin tricks, and they can be learned easily. Equally important, these tricks are entertaining. I will tell you precisely how to perform each one, explaining in detail every aspect. Where appropriate, I provide hints on appropriate "patter."

I perform these tricks, and I've taught them. You may not want to learn all of them, of course. But I'm sure you'll enjoy performing the ones you do learn.

Advanced coin manipulators can perform amazing feats of skill. For example, they can palm several coins in either hand, roll several coins over their knuckles, and actually palm coins on the *back* of the fingers. Far from denigrating these skills, I'm dazzled by them. But the bottom line is still *effect*. Here you will learn nearly every effect possible, using relatively easy sleights.

Tips

Unlike card tricks, most coin tricks are over in a few seconds. Very little patter is required, but this doesn't mean *no* patter. Prepare a little something to say for each trick.

For almost every trick, smoothness, *not speed*, is essential. So remember: *Don't hurry. Be deliberate.*

Strive for graceful gestures in your presentation. For instance, if you show that the left hand no longer holds the coin that was placed there, open the hand one finger at a time, starting with the little finger. Avoid abrupt movements. When performing, let your hands *flow*.

Size of Coins

Readers from countries other than the United States

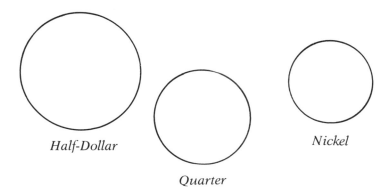

Half-Dollar

Quarter

Nickel

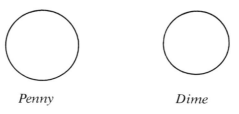

Penny   *Dime*

may find it useful to know the size of the coins referred to in this book.

· 1 ·

VANISHES

The magician shows a coin, and it disappears. This is unquestionably the basic coin trick. You should have several ways to accomplish this. But, from the spectators' point of view, one disappearance is pretty much the same as another. In most instances, you apparently place a coin in one hand, but actually you don't. You may be enchanted by the notion that each succeeding disappearance is more ingenious and more skillful. Spectators won't be captivated; they'll feel that you've performed the same trick several times.

What's important is the *reappearance* of the coin. Here you can get variety and retain audience interest. I offer many suggestions, and I'm sure that you'll come up with some ideas of your own.

French Drop

One of the oldest of all coin sleights is the *French Drop*. Many people are familiar with it. Done properly, it's an effective, deceptive vanish.

For most of these tricks, the type of coin or coins you use is irrelevant. I recommend, however, that you use a fairly large coin, either a quarter or a half-dollar, when you manipulate a single coin.

Let's try the basic sleight.

With the left hand turned palm up and fingers curled in, hold the coin between the first two fingers and the thumb.

The right hand is palm down as it approaches from above (Illus. 1). The right thumb is beneath the coin

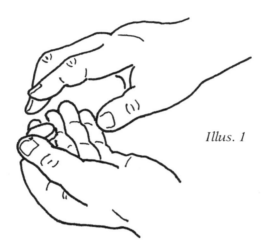

Illus. 1

and the fingers above it, and you close your right hand into a fist as you, presumably, take the coin.

Actually, you simply spread the first finger and thumb of the left hand slightly apart, dropping the coin onto the cupped fingers of the left hand. The right hand, which now supposedly holds the coin, continues to move forward (Illus. 2).

This is one of the simplest coin sleights and probably the best known, but the vast majority of those who attempt it do it badly. Perhaps you've seen someone perform the sleight and present both closed fists, asking you to pick out the one containing the coin.

Sleights should be performed smoothly and naturally. How do you learn to perform a sleight *naturally*?

Practise by actually taking the coin in your right fist instead of performing the sleight. Next, perform the *French Drop*. Then, actually take the coin. Continue alternating until, when you perform the sleight, you precisely duplicate the action of taking the coin. I don't

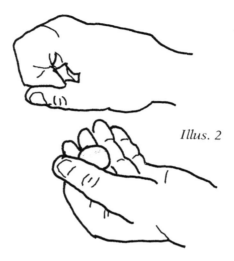

Illus. 2

recommend practising in front of a mirror (some performers tend to narrow their eyes so they won't see the sleight, and carry this habit over into performance), but do check periodically to see if the sleight looks natural. Be sure to try *both* ways in front of the mirror.

You've performed the *French Drop*, and the right fist has moved forward, ostensibly with the coin. What about that left hand? There's a tendency to want to hide the coin, to close the left hand; resist that temptation. Simply drop the cupped left hand naturally to your side. *Don't close the hand*; there's no need to, since the coin is secure there. No one will see it; attention is on the right hand. *But* the coin had better be produced, and soon.

Here's another possibility. Immediately after you ostensibly take the coin with the right hand, point to the right hand with the left forefinger, and then let the hand drop to your side.

The *French Drop* is perfect for *Up One Sleeve and Down the Other*, which you'll find in the section *Reappearances*, beginning on page 23.

French Drop for One

This is a mystifying variation of the *French Drop*, but it's best performed for an audience of one. Ideally, the spectator will be seated and you'll be standing. Otherwise, you'd have to hold the coin rather high, because it must be held close to the spectator's eye level.

The coin (preferably a fifty-cent piece) is held between the thumb and first finger of the palm-up left hand, about a foot from the spectator.

The right hand approaches from above, and the tips of the right second and third fingers push against the right side of the coin, pivoting it around (Illus. 3).

Illus. 3

As you complete the revolution of the coin (heads is now where tails was) several things happen. You loosen your grip on the coin with the left thumb and first finger, and the coin drops onto the cupped fingers of the left hand, and you press your right thumb against the right second and third fingers as though holding the coin.

Raise the right hand in the air, with the back of your hand to the spectator. Snap your fingers, showing that the coin has disappeared. With your left hand, produce the coin with one of the methods given in *Reappearances*, beginning on page 23.

Easy Vanish

There are several ways of pretending to place a coin in one hand while actually retaining it in the other. The following method is one of the easiest to perform, yet it's completely deceptive.

Any size coin will do for this stunt. First, practise the actual placement of the coin, then do the sleight.

Hold both hands out face up, a coin resting on the pads of the second and third fingers of the right hand.

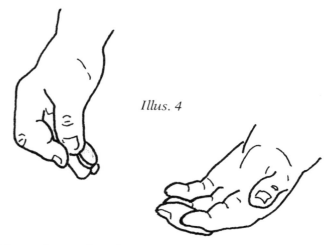

Illus. 4

Move the right thumb so that it holds the coin in place, turn the hand palm down and raise the hand so that it's above and to the right of the left hand (Illus. 4).

Place the coin in the middle of the left palm.

Let go of the coin, and as you withdraw the right hand, fingers still together, close the fingers of the left hand on the coin. As your right hand withdraws, the closing fingers of the left hand should brush lightly against the back of the right fingers (Illus. 5).

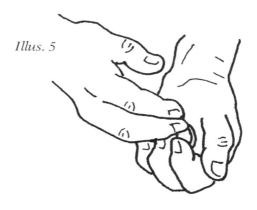

Illus. 5

When your right hand is a few inches from your left hand, cup the second, third, and fourth fingers, leaving the first finger extended. Tap your left wrist once with your right forefinger, and let your right hand drop naturally to your side. Gradually open the left hand, and, sure enough, the coin is there.

Practise the actual placement several times before you attempt the sleight. Do it very deliberately. You could do a leisurely two-count. Count "one" for placing the coin in the palm, and "two" for tapping the wrist with the forefinger.

For the sleight, you do everything in exactly the same way, except that at the step where you let go of the coin, simply hang on to it; keep it between the thumb and the second and third fingers of the right hand. Don't forget to tap your wrist with your forefinger; this creates the impression that your right hand is empty. Let your right hand drop to your side.

Now the closed left hand presumably holds the coin, but the coin is actually in the right hand. All that remains is the disclosure of the disappearance, followed instantly by a magical reappearance.

Easy Vanish is an excellent choice for *Cough It Up*, page 27, and *A Quick Gag*, page 28.

Thumb-Palm Vanish

At first, this sleight may seem a bit daunting. Like the others, however, it isn't very difficult. It may take just a bit more practice than some of the other vanishes.

You'll do a sleight called the *Thumb Palm*. But, as with other sleights, speed is not required, just smoothness and timing.

Hold the coin between the first and second fingers of the right hand, your other fingers folded in (Illus. 6).

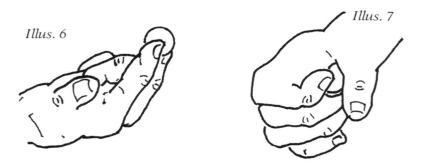

Illus. 7

Illus. 6

Bend the first two fingers all the way in, bringing the coin into the fork of the thumb and the first finger (Illus. 7).

Move the thumb towards the first finger, clipping the coin. Instantly extend the first two fingers (Illus. 8).

These moves by themselves don't constitute a vanish, of course. So here's the vanish.

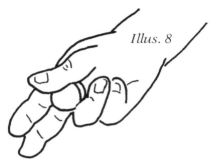

Illus. 8

Hold the coin between the first two fingers of the right hand. The left hand is held palm out and fingers down. Hold the coin in front of the left palm (Illus. 9).

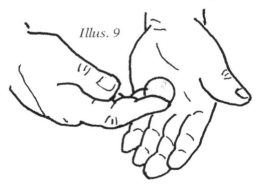

Illus. 9

The left hand revolves so that its back is to the audience and it conceals the back of the right hand (Illus. 10). As it does so, perform the *Thumb Palm* with the right hand. The move is completely covered by the left hand.

Instantly slide the right hand towards the ends of the right fingers. Close the fingers of the left hand around the extended fingers of the right hand (Illus. 11).

Pull the left fist away. Presumably, it now holds the coin.

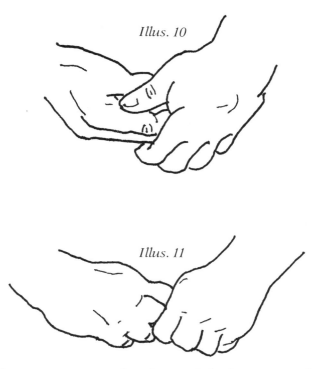

Illus. 10

Illus. 11

After you practise this for a while, be sure to check it out in front of the mirror. Use this vanish with *Pass Through the Legs*, on page 25.

Basic Vanish

This elementary vanishing sleight is totally convincing. First, the legitimate move.

Hold out both hands, palms up. A coin is in the precise center of the right palm.

Your right hand approaches the left from slightly below. The bottom of the right palm moves upward so that it touches the back of the tips of the left fingers (Illus. 12).

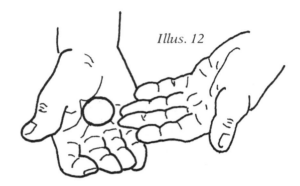

Illus. 12

Drop the coin into the left palm as your right hand moves back, closing the fingers of the left hand (Illus. 13).

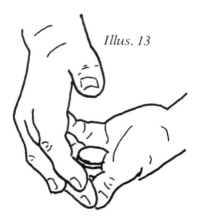

Illus. 13

Continue moving the right hand back several inches, and then drop that hand naturally to your side. The entire move should be done rapidly and *smoothly*.

Now for the sleight. You should probably use a coin no smaller than a quarter. Place the coin in the center of your right palm. Now close the fingers and thumb slightly, gripping the coin (Illus. 14). Congratulations! You have just *palmed a coin*!

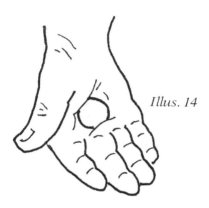

Illus. 14

With a little practice, you'll get a feel for placing the coin in exactly the right position for performing the palm. When you take the coin into your right hand and turn both hands palm up, don't be shy about not having the coin in the proper position. Bounce the coin up and down until it settles into the ideal place.

To perform the sleight, your right hand with the coin in its palm approaches the left hand from slightly below, as shown in Illus. 12. The minute the back of the right hand is to the audience, however, squeeze the fingers and thumb slightly, performing the palm. When you close the left hand with the right, you retain the coin in the palm of the right hand, which drops to your side.

As before, practise doing the actual drop and then the sleight. From time to time, check yourself in the mirror.

The *Basic Vanish* is ideal for *Catch as Catch Can*, on page 28, and it is the preferred sleight for *Vanish into Thin Air*, on page 31.

Basic Vanish (Variation)

Refer back to Illus. 12. The right hand, holding the palmed coin, approaches the left from slightly below and touches the back of the tips of the left fingers. In this version, however, the right hand rests on the *pads* of the left fingers (Illus. 15).

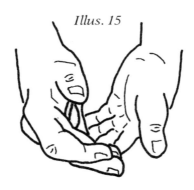

Illus. 15

Everything else is the same. The coin is presumably dropped as the left fingers close and the right hand moves towards the body. Try both versions and use the one which works best for you.

Combined Vanish

This vanish blends elements of the *Easy Vanish* and the *Basic Vanish*. For certain tricks, the following vanish is the sleight of choice, for instance, for *Leg Work*, on page 36.

Again, both hands are displayed, palms up. A coin lies on the right fingers approximately ½" from the tips. Bring the right hand over, and in front of, the left hand, with the tips of the right fingers under and touching the back of the tips of the left fingers (Illus. 16).

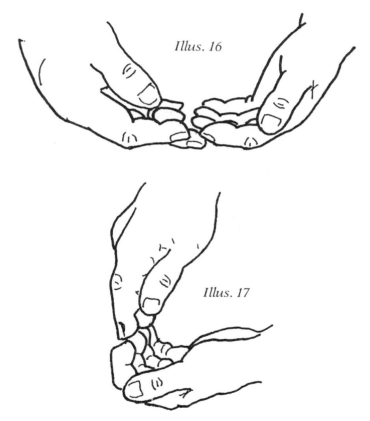

Illus. 16

Illus. 17

As the right hand moves up and back, closing the left fingers and presumably dropping the coin, the right thumb grips the coin (Illus. 17).

The right hand continues back a few inches. Cup the second, third, and fourth fingers of the right hand and tap the left wrist with the extended forefinger. In some tricks, this last tapping move may be omitted.

· 2 ·

REAPPEARANCES

You can use most of these reappearances with any vanish.

Slap Through the Leg

Let's assume that you've pretended to place a coin in your left hand in one of the vanishes. Do *not* immediately show the left hand empty. Instead, place your right hand under your right leg and slap the top of that leg with an open left hand. *Now* show that your left hand is empty, and produce the coin with your right hand from behind the leg.

If you have performed the *French Drop* (page 9), pretending to take the coin with the *right* hand, simply reverse the hands in the above description.

From a Spectator's Ear

Suppose that you've performed the *French Drop* (page 9). You've presumably taken the coin with your right hand, whereas it is actually in the left. Raise your right hand, held in a loose fist, above shoulder level (as though you were holding the coin up), letting your left hand drop naturally to your side. Then snap the fingers of the right hand. Turn the palm towards the audience, showing that your right hand is empty.

Produce the coin from a spectator's ear. Simply reach towards the spectator's ear with your cupped left hand, the back of your hand towards the spectators. When you are about an inch or so from the spectator's ear, slide the coin to your fingertips with your thumb, and almost touch the ear with the coin. Instantly, push the coin into sight as you pull the hand away from the ear.

Another way to show that the coin has vanished is to drop the right hand to belt level and make an upward tossing movement, as though throwing the coin into the air. You can then produce the coin from the spectator's ear.

Pass Through the Head _____

This reappearance may be used with any vanish. Suppose that you've pretended to place a coin in your left hand, whereas it is actually in your right hand.

Approach a spectator. Reach out with your left hand, back of the hand towards the audience, pretending to hold the coin between your thumb and fingertips. Lightly push your fingers against the side of his head above his ear.

Meanwhile, you have let the coin drop onto the fingers of the right hand. Reach out with your right hand, its *back* to the spectators, so that they can't see that you hold the coin between fingers and thumb. *Immediately* after you have pushed against the side of the spectator's head with the left hand, produce the coin at your fingertips from the corresponding spot at the other side of his head using your right hand.

Pass Through the Legs _____

Again, any vanish may be used. You might use the *Thumb-Palm Vanish* (page 15), in which you've presumably taken the coin in your left fist, although you actually retain it in a thumb palm in your right hand.

After pulling the left fist from the right fingers, slap your left hand against the side of your left leg. Instantly, slap your right hand against the side of your right leg and display the coin at your fingertips, showing that the coin has penetrated both legs.

Up One Sleeve and Down the Other _____

Although you may do this reappearance with any vanish, try it with the *French Drop* (page 9). In this description, assume that you're using the *French Drop*.

To perform this trick, wear a suit jacket or a long-sleeved shirt or blouse.

Playing with a coin, tossing it from hand to hand, say something like, "As you must know, many magicians are capable of making objects disappear by sending them up their sleeves. I'd like to show you how this is done."

At this point, you're holding the coin in your left hand. Duplicating the action of the *French Drop*, take the coin into your right hand. Openly show it and then turn your hand down in the position shown in Illus. 18.

"I want to show you how they do this with a coin. They hold it in the fingers like this. And then they move the hand forward quite rapidly. The coin slides off the fingers and goes up the sleeve."

Slowly move your right hand forward, illustrating how the coin is sent up the sleeve.

Toss the coin into your left hand and hold it in the same "sleeving" position as you did with your right hand.

"You can do it with either hand, of course. It's all in the forward movement."

Move the left hand slowly forward, showing how the coin is sleeved.

Hold the coin in the left hand in the *French Drop* position. As you continue to talk, perform the *French Drop*, presumably taking the coin in your right hand.

"Now I'll show you the stunt in action."

You have performed the *French Drop* and you are holding your right hand in the "sleeving" position shown in Illus. 18. Your left hand has fallen naturally to

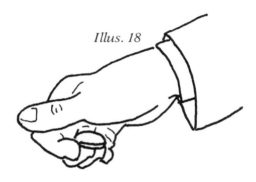

Illus. 18

your side. Jerk your right hand forward, supposedly sending the coin up your sleeve.

"See? You get the coin up your sleeve easily enough. But I'll show you something even tougher."

Raise your right arm out to the side and shake it. Then hunch your shoulders up and down several times as you say:

"The real trick is to get it to go up the arm . . . across the shoulders . . ."

Jerk your left arm up and down a few times.

". . . over to the other sleeve . . . and into the other hand."

Do a little catching movement with your hanging left arm and then show the coin. You have apparently managed a very difficult feat.

This is a most entertaining trick. Most will be deceived, but even those who aren't will be amused by your daring and by your gyrations.

Cough It Up

You could use any vanish with this trick, but try the *Easy Vanish* (page 13). This reappearance provides a little drama and a touch of humor.

Before performing the sleight, bend over so that people can see the top of your head. Touch the middle of your head, saying:

"I don't know if you can see it from there, but I have a little hole in the top of my head. Yes, people are right about me, but it does come in handy now and then."

Perform the *Easy Vanish*. Then bring your left hand above your head and open the fingers as you slap the top of your head. *Immediately*, bring your right hand to your mouth as if to cover a cough, and let your left hand drop to stomach level. Cough, and let the coin fall from your right hand, catching the coin in your left hand.

The trick usually gets a laugh, and *always* delights children.

You may wish to indicate the hole in the top of your head *after* the vanish. Simply touch the middle of your pate with the right forefinger as you explain about the hole, and then complete the trick as above. This handling, while less direct, apparently demonstrates that your right hand is empty.

A Quick Gag

If you are the sort who likes to execute the small practical joke, you might try this variation of the *Easy Vanish* (page 13); most of the other vanishes will also do. When you are paying for a purchase with a coin, show the coin in your right hand, perform the *Easy Vanish*, and then slap your left hand on the counter in front of the clerk. At the exact instant that your hand hits the counter, hit the counter in front of you with the coin in your right hand. The illusion is perfect. Lift your left hand, showing that the coin is not there; then push the coin to the clerk with your right hand.

Catch as Catch Can

This excellent method of retrieving a vanished coin is deceptively easy to perform. The timing must be precise, however. Spend as much time practising this as you would spend on a difficult sleight.

Using any vanish, pretend to place a coin in the left hand. Since the coin must be held in the palm of the right hand, the *Basic Vanish* (page 17) works well.

The left hand is closed; the right hand holds a coin in the palm. Raise both hands to head level, backs of the hands towards the spectators. The fingers of the right hand should be spread. Don't worry about the coin; it will stay in the right palm, unseen and quite secure.

Make an upward throwing motion with the left hand, spreading the fingers. Follow the flight of the invisible coin with your eyes, asking, "Where'd it go?"

Make a quarter-turn to the left as you do three things: Turn the left hand so that the palm is towards the audience, fingers still spread. Drop the right hand to waist level, letting the coin fall onto the left fingers. With the left hand, reach to the left and grab the invisible coin, saying, "Here!"

Quickly bring the left fist down towards the right hand and, when the left fist is about a foot away from the right hand, make a throwing motion, as though tossing the coin into the right hand. Instantly, move the right hand slightly upward, bouncing the coin an inch or so into the air, simulating the catching of the coin, followed by a little bounce. Display the coin at the fingertips, both hands held up, palms towards the audience.

The little bounce when you catch the coin in the right hand is critical. The audience sees the coin hop into view as though it had just arrived. Practise the timing.

Behind the Knee

Very few reappearances can match this one. A coin disappears. You attempt to pull it from your leg using your empty left hand; no luck. You try from the right side of your leg with your empty right hand; still no luck. You try with the left hand again, and there's the coin!

You may use any vanish to (ostensibly) place a coin in your left hand, while retaining the coin in your right hand. The right hand drops casually to your side, as the left hand is shown to be empty.

Immediately drop the left hand, palm outward, to slightly behind the left knee, where you grip a little fabric of your trousers between your fingers and thumb. Apparently, you are trying to pull the coin from the fabric. Let the fabric slide through your fingers, showing that your hand is empty. Return the hand to slightly behind the knee.

You have let the coin drop so that it's resting on the fingers of your right hand. With the back of your right hand to the audience, bring your right hand to the rear of the right side of the knee. Again, you are going to grip the fabric of your trousers. Before you do this, pass the coin to the fingers of the left hand. Simply drop the coin off the ends of your right fingers as you grip the fabric. The coin falls onto the tips of the left fingers, which hold it against the back of the knee.

Pull out the fabric with the right hand, trying to extract the coin. Let the hand slide off, showing that it's empty.

Try again with the left hand. As you pull out the fabric, the coin is held behind it. Gradually, pull the coin out (Illus. 19).

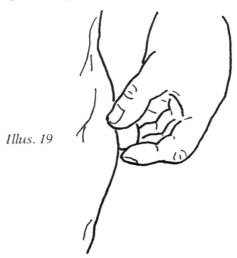

Illus. 19

Apparently, you have shown both hands empty, but you've then produced the coin.

· 3 ·

COMPLETE VANISHES

In other "vanishes" and "reappearances," a coin is apparently in one hand but it's actually in the other. But in *complete* vanishes a coin disappears altogether.

Vanish into Thin Air

Before you can perform this astounding coin disappearance, you must master the *Basic Vanish* (page 17). You'll pass a coin through your legs twice, and then cause it to vanish into thin air.

The one requirement is that no one can be behind you. Wear a suit jacket or its equivalent. As you will see, the jacket should not be buttoned. There will be alternatives later on to wearing a suit jacket.

Stand facing the audience. Flip the coin in the air a few times and then take it in the palm of your right hand.

Perform the *Basic Vanish*.

Turn so that your left side is to the audience. Lift your left leg slightly and slap your closed left hand against the side of your knee.

Immediately turn so that your right side is towards the audience. Lift your right leg slightly and slap your closed right hand against the side of your knee. Raise your right hand high in the air, its back towards the audience, and show the coin at your fingertips. Apparently, the coin has passed right through your legs. Again take the coin in the palm of your right hand.

Perform the movement of the *Basic Vanish*, *but actually drop the coin into the left hand*.

Turn your left side towards the audience and slap your left hand against the side of your knee.

Turn your right side towards the audience and slap your right hand against the side of your knee. As you do so, drop the coin from the left hand into the side pocket of your jacket.

As before, raise your right hand in the air, its back towards the audience, as though you were displaying the coin. Turn so that you face the audience. Close your right hand into a fist as you drop your hand to chest level, and then perform a tossing motion into the air, as though you were throwing the coin towards the ceiling. The coin has vanished. Show both hands. Your audience will be completely baffled. If you are going to perform more coin tricks, take a coin from some *other* pocket.

What if you're not wearing a suit jacket? You can drop the coin into your pants pocket, or you could tuck the coin under the waist of your pants or skirt. A sweater with side pockets will also do, of course.

The Little Coin That Wasn't There

Let's suppose that you've demonstrated your skill and magical powers with a number of coin tricks, and you feel that the time has come to call it quits. The only requirement for the following trick is that you have several small coins in your left pants pocket or purse. A few nickels, a few dimes, and several pennies would be perfect.

Put away any other coins that you've been working with, preferably in your right pants pocket. If this is your last trick of the session, you'll want to close with nothing to be picked up and put away.

With your left hand, remove the coins from your purse or left pants pocket. Hold them out in your palm as you poke through them with the right fingers, apparently seeking the proper coin.

Say, "This dime will do." You can name any of the coins; it doesn't matter. Raising your left hand slightly, apparently pick up the coin between the second and third fingers and the thumb of the right hand. Actually, you pick up nothing. Hold the hand, however, as though you actually have a coin (Illus. 20). Put the coins back into your pocket or purse.

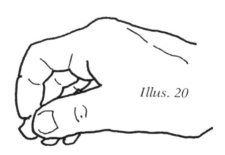

Illus. 20

Immediately, go through the motions of placing the nonexistent coin into your left hand. Use one of the regular vanish moves. You could use the *Easy Vanish*, in which you tap the left wrist with the right first finger after presumably placing the coin in the left hand. Normally, you would drop your right hand to your side, but for this trick, keep the right hand stiffly pointing at the left hand, because you want people to notice that right hand.

Tap your left fingers and then open them, showing that the coin has disappeared. Keep your right hand held stiffly near the left. Someone is bound to notice and ask to see what you have in your right hand. Slowly open the fingers, showing that your right hand is also empty. Show both sides of your hands and shrug. Few tricks provide as good an effect for such a small amount of work.

· 4 ·

VARIOUS TRICKS

Clink! _____

The effectiveness of this trick depends upon two coins making a loud "clink" as they hit together. The best approach is to use two fifty-cent pieces.

Both coins are resting on a table. Pick up one with the right hand. Perform the *Basic Vanish* (page 17), ostensibly placing the coin in your left hand.

Retain the coin in the palm position in the right hand, and then use that same (right) hand to pick up the second coin between the second and third fingers and thumb.

The second coin rests on the second and third fingers as the right hand approaches the left from above (Illus. 21).

The left hand partially opens to accept the dropped coin. Instead of dropping the coin from your fingers, release the coin from the palm. As the coin falls into your left hand, it clinks against the coin balanced on your second and third fingers. Your left fingers close immediately.

Without moving your fingers, drop your right hand to your side. At the same time, drop your left hand to your side. Make a quick up-and-down move with both hands. Show both hands. One coin has jumped to the right hand.

The clinking sound is very deceptive. The strong impression is created that the second coin has struck the first coin when the second fell into your left hand.

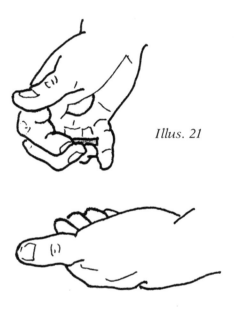

Illus. 21

Leg Work

For this trick, the *Combined Vanish* works best. See page 20.

Place your left foot on a chair. Or, if you have an excellent sense of balance, you could raise your knee in the air. Another possibility is to be seated in a chair.

Place a coin—preferably a penny—on your raised left leg near the knee, and another several inches nearer your torso.

Place the back of your open left hand on top of the nearer coin (the one closer to your torso).

Pick up the other coin and pretend to place it in your left hand, using the *Combined Vanish* (or one· of the other vanishes). As you move your right hand away, let the coin fall onto your cupped fingers, so that you will be able to pick up the other coin between your first finger and thumb.

Raise your closed left hand to your mouth, and blow into your left fist. *At precisely the same time*, pick up the other coin with the first finger and thumb of your right hand.

Hold both hands in front of you in two fists, separated by a foot or so. Revolve both hands slowly several times, and then open them, showing that both coins are in your right hand.

As you perform this trick, you might want to say:

"Like people, coins are sometimes attracted to each other. Here we have two coins, complete strangers, as far as I know."

By this time, you should be ready to show the two coins in your right hand.

"But look. Apparently, there was real magnetism between them."

This trick shouldn't be done speedily. Strive for smoothness and naturalness. The moves should flow. When the moves become automatic, you can perform several repetitions without fear of discovery.

Why does this trick work? Blowing into the left fist while picking up the coin with the right hand tends to confuse spectators. They simply can't follow what you're doing.

Throwback

Display a coin in your right hand. Point to it with your left hand.

Swing both arms down so that they go slightly behind your back, and then instantly swing them up again, your right hand tossing the coin into the air about two feet or so. Both hands are back to the audience. Your left hand has its first finger extended so that it can point to the coin which has been tossed into the air.

Your right hand catches the coin, and both arms swing down again, going behind your back. Again the coin is tossed into the air and caught by your right hand as your left first finger points.

When your hands swing behind your back the third time, the coin is tossed from your right hand to your left. Both hands come up as before, and the invisible coin is tossed into the air, with your left first finger pointing.

In great puzzlement, look at your empty right hand as you show its palm to the audience. At the same time, let your left hand drop to your side, fingers loosely curled around the coin. *Immediately*, say, "Ah, there it is!" With your right hand, reach to a spectator's left ear as though to produce the coin. Close your fingers and thumb as though grasping the coin. Then, looking puzzled, show the hand empty. "Wait a minute," you say, as you reach out with your left hand and produce the coin from his right ear.

There are other possible conclusions. You could do the conclusion of *Catch as Catch Can* (page 28), for instance, reversing the hands. Or you could do *Behind the Knee*, on page 29.

Seven Cents

You need seven pennies for this trick. This trick can be repeated several times; no particular skill is required.

Show that your hands are empty. Give seven pennies to a spectator. Have him verify that there are only seven.

Take the pennies back and hold them in your cupped left hand. Say to the spectator:

"I'd like you to hold out your left hand so that we can check the count. When I've placed the seventh penny in your hand, I want you to close your hand immediately so that no pennies can escape. Ready?"

Pick up a penny with your right hand, holding it between your second finger and thumb. Your hand should be *palm down* as you place the penny into the palm of the spectator's hand, counting, "One." Place another penny into his hand the same way, making sure that you clink it against the penny already there. As you do so, count, "Two." Continue in the same way with pennies three, four, and five.

Place the sixth penny into his hand in the same way, counting, "Six." Make sure to clink it against one of the coins, *but withdraw your hand, retaining the coin.* Since the back of your hand is to the spectators, no one will see that you still have the coin. Besides, your next move captures everyone's attention.

Immediately, with your left hand, toss the remaining coin into his hand, counting, "Seven." He should close his hand instantly. If he fails to do so, help him with the left hand by placing it beneath his fingers and pushing upward, saying, "Close your hand!"

Quickly show that your left hand is empty and tap his fingers with your left fingers. Bring your right hand under his left and push the coin against it. Bring your hand away, displaying the penny at your fingertips. It's as though you had pulled it through the back of his hand!

Tell the spectator:

"There seems to be a hole in your hand. Let's try it again."

Take the pennies and repeat the trick at least once. Repeating it three times is just about right.

Aspiring magicians have a tendency to feel that the move involved in this trick is much too bold, and that they won't get away with it. At the time you keep the penny, all attention is on the delivery of the seventh coin and the closing of the hand.

The key is to keep a consistent rhythm as you count the coins into the spectator's hand. The sixth coin should be counted out in precisely the same way as the first five.

This is a very difficult trick to practise, since it's difficult to duplicate the actual action by placing coins on a table, for instance. You'll probably have to rehearse with a trusted friend. Don't be surprised if you fool your friend on your first try!

Quick Transpo _____

This trick is fast and effective. A coin held under one hand magically moves under the other hand. Two versions of this trick appear in the book. *Quick Transpo* (page 40) is somewhat easier, and it's done standing up. The other, *Hand to Hand*, appears on page 51.

Flip a coin (any size) into the air a few times to keep spectators from focusing on the key move. Hold both hands out and palms up, displaying the coin in the right hand about ½" from the ends of the fingers.

Simultaneously slap your two hands against your stomach, tossing the coin from the right hand so that it lands under the left. Because of the simultaneous movement of the hands, the coin arrives just before the left hand smacks against your stomach (Illus. 22).

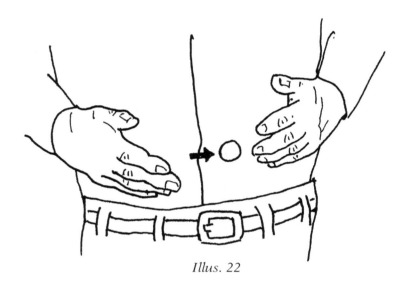

Illus. 22

Rub your right hand against your stomach vigorously, as though rubbing the coin away. Remove your right hand from your stomach and show that it is empty. Turn over your left hand, letting the coin drop into it. Display the coin.

Don't hesitate to try this trick. There's a good chance that you will succeed in a good throw on your first attempt. You'll get the knack in less than five minutes.

Bill Fold

A coin is folded into a dollar bill. With no suspicious

moves (and no particular skill on the part of the performer), the coin disappears. This trick has many versions. Ordinarily, a piece of paper would be used for
the fold. A dollar bill may be more readily available.

Take out a dollar bill and a nickel, or borrow them
from trusting spectators. As you will see, the climax
will work better if you borrow the dollar bill.

Place the nickel in the center of the dollar bill, and
display the bill, holding your left thumb on top of the
nickel (Illus. 23).

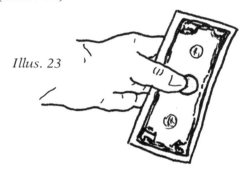

Illus. 23

You will fold the nickel into the dollar bill, and then
you'll open the folds and show that the coin is still
there. Then you'll refold the dollar bill in a tricky way.
It's important that you seem to fold the bill in precisely
the same way both times.

The side of the bill on which you are holding the
nickel faces you. With your right hand, fold down and
inward the top third of the bill, covering the coin. Grip
the right side of the coin through the bill with your
right thumb, letting go with the left thumb (Illus. 24).
Slide the bill and coin upwards with the right hand,
through the fingers and thumb of the left hand. The
left hand should now be at the bottom of the bill, in
position to fold the bottom third of the bill up and
inward. Do so (Illus. 25).

Now fold in the two sides of the bill so that the nickel has about ¼″ of leeway on each side (Illus. 26).

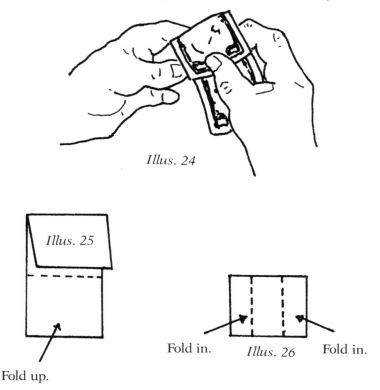

Illus. 24

Illus. 25

Fold up.

Fold in.   *Illus. 26*   Fold in.

Toss the packet on the table, so that it makes a clunk.

Pick up the packet, saying, "No, no, the coin is actually here." Unwrap the packet and take out the coin, displaying it in your *left* hand between your thumb and fingers.

Replace the coin in the center of the dollar bill, again holding it in place with your left thumb. As before, fold the top third of the bill down and inward, but *don't* transfer your grip on the coin to your right thumb. Instead, slide the bill up with your right hand. The coin naturally slides down to the lower third of the bill (Illus. 27). Tilt the packet slightly back towards you as you fold the bottom third up and inward. The coin, of course, is inside this last fold.

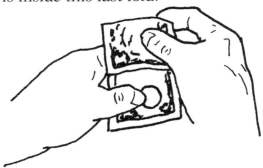

Now fold in the two sides of the bill exactly as you did before. Unknown to the audience, the coin is resting in a chute, and it will drop out if you simply turn the packet around.

Toss the packet on the table so that the packet makes a clunk. Don't fear; the coin *won't* come out.

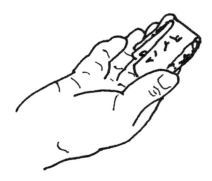

Pick up the packet in your right hand, with the opening of the "chute" at the bottom. Display the packet, holding it loosely between your fingers and thumb (Illus. 28). Let the coin drop into your hand. As you display the packet, say:

"Does anyone have a match or a lighter?"

The spectator who loaned the dollar may display some disapproval. In any case, address him:

"You don't want me to do it that way? All right, we'll try something else."

Take the packet in your left hand and hold it in a loose fist. Let your right hand drop naturally to your side in a cupped position. Leaning over, place your left hand on a table, the hand still in a loose fist, palm down. Reach under the table with your right hand. Knock your left hand three times on the table. At the third knock, bring forth your right hand, showing the nickel. Drop it on the table. Very carefully unfold the dollar bill and show it to your audience.

An alternative conclusion is to pick up the packet with your right hand as before, but with the opening of the "chute" at the top. Hold your shirt pocket or top jacket pocket open with your left hand. As you bring the packet to the pocket, turn the packet over, and start to put the packet into the pocket. As you do so, say to the spectator who loaned you the bill, "Do you mind if I keep this?" You place the packet only ½" or so into your pocket, spilling the coin in, and then you instantly withdraw the packet.

"All right, all right. Do you mind if I give it away?"

Before the spectator responds, add:

"Wait, I have a better idea. Let's give the nickel away."

Unfold the bill, showing that the coin has disappeared.

"Oh, well. A nickel isn't worth much anyway."

Pocket Penetration

You place a coin in your pants pocket. It magically penetrates right through the cloth.

For this trick you are going to have to perform the *Thumb-Palm Vanish*, on page 15.

A half-dollar is best for this trick. Display the coin between the first and second fingers of your right hand. This is the position which precedes the *Thumb Palm*. Make about a quarter-turn to the left so that your right side is somewhat towards the audience. In a sweeping movement, bring your right hand behind and above your right-hand pants pocket. While doing this, perform the *Thumb Palm*. In the same motion, thrust your right hand into your pocket. The large sweeping motion makes the *Thumb Palm* undetectable. You're now holding your right hand in your pocket, apparently with a half-dollar at your fingertips; actually it is "thumb-palmed."

Place your left fingers on the outside of your pocket at a point slightly beyond the ends of your right fingers. Presumably, you're holding the coin from outside the pocket.

Withdraw your right hand from your pocket and, as you turn to the front, let the coin drop onto your right fingers. Naturally, the back of your hand is to your audience.

Move your left hand away as you slap the coin against your trousers, a few inches below where your left hand had been.

Slide your right thumb under the coin and pinch a portion of cloth between your thumb and the coin. Lifting upwards, fold the cloth over the coin as you turn the coin over. Withdraw your right hand as you place your left fingertips on top of the fold, holding the coin in place.

Snap the fingers of your right hand. With your right fingers, grab a pinch of trousers a few inches below the coin. Gradually pull the cloth down, allowing the coin to slowly slide into sight.

After a bit more than half of the coin is revealed, take the coin with your right fingers and pull out the coin the rest of the way. Smooth your trousers using your left hand, showing that there is no hole in your trousers. Display the coin at your right fingertips.

The Back of My Hand

Display a fifty-cent piece at your fingertips, with the back of your hand towards the audience. Your left hand is held in a knuckles-down fist (Illus. 29).

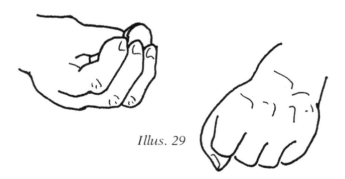

Illus. 29

Push the coin against the back of your left hand, letting your fingers slip over the coin, so that the coin is no longer visible (Illus. 30).

Drop your right hand several inches below your left. Eagerly open your left hand, and express disappointment that your left hand is empty.

Saying, "I'll try again," swing the right hand into the air, supposedly to display the coin again, as you did the first time. Actually, as your right hand swings

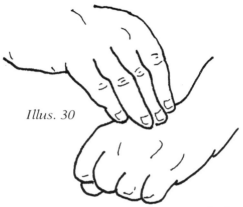

Illus. 30

upwards behind your left hand, your right hand lets go of the coin, and the coin will fall into your open left palm (Illus. 31). It's important that your eyes follow your right hand, so that all attention will be on it and the presumed coin. Again, hold your left hand in a knuckles-down fist.

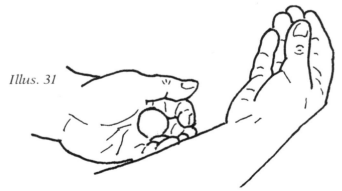

Illus. 31

Push against the back of your left hand, exactly as you did when you actually held the coin. Drop your right hand. Turn your left hand over, showing the coin.

· 5 ·

AT THE
TABLE

Seated at a table, the magician can perform some of the very best coin tricks.

Cross-Up

This trick can be done equally well sitting at a table, or leaning over one. Although this trick is quite easy to perform, it's extremely deceptive. You'll need either two half-dollars, or two quarters.

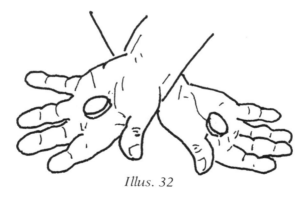

Illus. 32

Start with your hands crossed at the wrists, palms up. One coin is in each palm (Illus. 32).

Form your hands into loose fists and turn them over, keeping the wrists crossed (Illus. 33). As you form the fists, palm the coin which is in the right hand. This palm is explained in *Basic Vanish* on page 17.

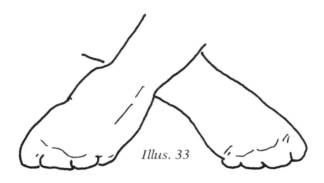

Illus. 33

Move both hands to the left, opening the left hand, dropping its coin to the table.

Still keeping your wrists crossed, pick up the coin with your left fingers and thumb. Form a loose fist, holding the coin on your fingertips.

Move your hands to the right. Simultaneously drop the coin from your left fingers (*without opening the hand*) and open your right hand, but retain the coin in your right palm.

Hands still crossed, pick up the coin on the table using your right fingers and thumb.

Slowly and deliberately separate your hands. Smack both fists on the table. Turn your hands over and open them, showing that the coins are now in the same hand.

Here's an alternative ending. Put your right hand under the table. Smack your left palm on the table. Shake the coins in your right hand so that there is at least one pronounced clink. Turn over your left hand

and lift it, showing that the coin is gone. Bring out your right hand, showing the two coins.

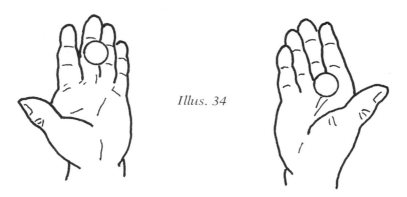

Illus. 34

Hand to Hand

This is a slightly more difficult version of *Quick Transpo*, on page 40. You'll show a coin in each hand, yet when you slap the coins down on the table, both will end up in the same hand.

Both hands are placed palms up on the table, a coin resting on each hand (Illus. 34). If you look at the illustration, you'll see that the coin in your right hand is on the right side of the hand, while the coin in your left hand is on the fingers. The positioning is important, for you're about to toss the coin from the right hand to the left hand, and you don't want a telltale clink. Also, placing the coin on the right side of the right hand makes it easier to throw the coin.

The two hands should be separated by a few inches more than the width of two hands.

With a quick movement, turn both hands over and inward, smacking them palms down on the table. As you do so, toss the coin from the right hand so that the coin lands under the descending left hand.

The technique of the throw is a bit tricky. As the proper method is described please remember that the entire move takes only a fraction of a second. Raise both hands about 2″ above the table before turning them inward and slapping them down. The coin is tossed as the palms face each other. The coin is slapped down, along with the other coin, with the left hand. Meanwhile, the right hand also smacks the table, right next to the left hand. Keep in mind that you must *throw* the coin from the right hand.

To end the trick, make a circular motion on the table with your right hand; then turn your right hand over and move it aside, showing that the coin has vanished. Lift your left hand, revealing both coins.

When done properly, the passage of the coin is absolutely invisible. About ten minutes of practice should do it.

The position of the coin in each hand has been emphasized. The trick can also be performed with both coins on the palms and both coins on the fingers. Experiment to find which method works best for you. The trick can be performed with any size of coin, up to a coin the size of a quarter.

Once you develop the proper timing, you can perform the trick with any small object—dice, poker chips, etc.

Leaping Pennies

You can do this trick while seated at a table, or leaning over one. It can even be done kneeling down on the carpet.

Despite its title, this trick can be done with any kind of coin, except fifty-cent pieces, which are too large.

Pennies are suggested because they are generally available. Make sure, however, that all the coins look alike.

The effect is extraordinary. Four pennies are held in each hand. One coin is deliberately transferred from the left hand to the right hand. The other three in the left hand invisibly follow, leaving none in the left hand and all eight in the right.

Surprisingly, the trick is quite easy, requiring no particular skill.

Place the eight pennies in two rows on a table. The rows should be about 4″ apart, and the pennies in each row about 3″ apart.

Say something like this:

"Eight pennies. I really hate to show off, but I'd like to demonstrate one of my proudest achievements. After years of practice, I've learned to count by twos."

Look around as though this announcement had been greeted by skepticism.

"All right, then; I'll *prove* it."

Hold the hands in loose fists, thumbs at the sides. Move the hands to the two coins nearest the spectators, holding your right hand to the right of the coin on the right side, and your left hand to the left of the coin on the left side.

Simultaneously, with each hand, pick up a coin between your first fingers and thumbs (Illus. 35).

Lift both hands a few inches above the table. In a throwing motion, bring your hands downwards and together, about 1″ apart. Let go of the coins so that they fall from the inner end of each hand. Continue with the motion by separating the hands about 12″. The entire move is continuous—hands down and together, coins dropped, hands separated, as shown by the arrows in Illus. 36.

As the coins are dropped, you say, "Two."

Pick up the two coins as before, and then pick up the two coins now nearest the spectators. Repeat the

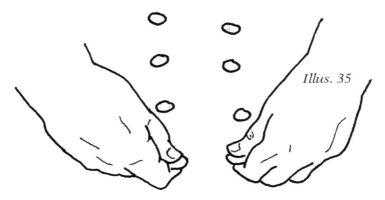

Illus. 35

downward throwing movement, only this time you let go of *both coins from the left hand,* retaining the two in your right hand. The illusion is that you have again dropped one coin from each hand. Make sure that both

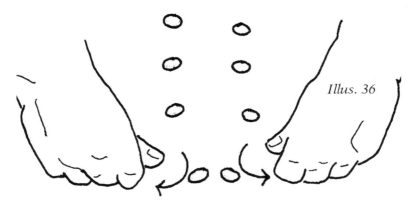

Illus. 36

hands still remain in a loose fist. Again, in a continuous motion, separate your hands about 12". As you drop the two coins from your left hand, say, "Four." Pick up the two coins, one in each hand.

With the next two coins on the table, you repeat the entire action described in the preceding paragraph. This time, of course, you say, "Six," when you drop both coins from your left hand.

Repeat, saying, "Eight," when you drop the coins. Pick up one coin in each hand, and hold the hands separated by several inches.

Spectators believe that you now hold four coins in each hand. In fact, you have one coin in the left hand and seven in the right.

Now you'll create the impression that you could equally well transport the coins to either hand. Say:

"Now let's play follow the leader. We'll take a coin from this hand . . ."

Push a coin out from your right hand (Illus. 37). Draw the coin back into your hand.

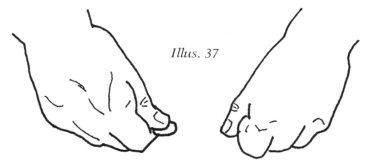

Illus. 37

"No, we'll take one from this hand . . ."

Push a coin out from your left hand. Very deliberately drop the coin on the table.

". . . and take it in the other."

Pick up the coin with the first finger and thumb of your right hand.

"Let's see if the other coins follow the leader."

Hold your hands separated by about 18". Make an up-and-down movement with both hands, letting the coins jingle in your right hand. Open your left hand, showing that it's empty. Open your right hand, showing that all the coins are there. Drop the coins on the table.

In other versions of this trick, the student is instructed to perform a sleight at the end, transferring the lone coin to the other hand. But, the trick is more effective when, as above, you let the single coin lead the way. A perfect follow-up to this trick would be *A Western Tale*, on page 99, which produces approximately the same effect, but it uses no sleights.

Through the Table _____

This is the simplest possible method of passing a coin through a table.

You are seated at a table. Ostensibly place a coin in your left hand, but actually retain it in your right, using either the *Basic Vanish* (page 17), or *Basic Vanish (Variation)*, on page 20.

Extend your closed left hand so that it rests on the table. Let your right hand drop casually onto your lap, and place the coin on your leg. As you talk, bring your right hand up and gesture with it, casually showing that it's empty. Here's what to say:

"I have noticed that the molecules in wood are not nearly so dense as the molecules in metal. Sometimes, under the right conditions, we can take advantage of that by passing metal *through* wood. Like this!"

Slap your left palm down on the table as you drop your right hand to your lap. Pick up the coin with your right hand and immediately move your right hand under the table. Arrange to have the coin at your right fingertips as you bring the coin out from under the table and display it.

Under the Table

One coin passes through the table to join another. Any two coins may be used. No special skill is required, but the timing must be exact.

Begin by saying:

"I don't know if you can see it, but there's a small hole in the table. I hope it doesn't cause a problem here."

Hold your left hand palm up on the table and place a coin in that palm. Another coin is to the right of this, and your right hand rests on the table near it (Illus. 38).

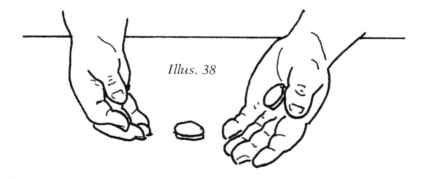

Illus. 38

You must perform two actions simultaneously.

(1) The coin on the table is drawn to the edge of the table by the fingers of the right hand. The right thumb grasps the underside of the coin as it clears the edge. Thus, the coin is held between fingers and thumb.

(2) Your left hand turns over inward and slaps its coin down exactly where the other coin had been.

Return the left hand to its palm-up position and immediately place the coin that's in your right hand into your left palm. *Instantly* repeat the action of the preceding two paragraphs, drawing the coin off the table and slapping your left hand down with its coin in the same place as the other coin had been. Repeat at least one more time.

For the fourth time, draw the coin off the table and slap the other coin down. When the coin you draw with the right hand reaches the edge of the table, simply drop that coin into your lap. Your left hand returns to its palm-up position, and your right hand pretends to place a coin in it, in precisely the same fashion as before. As before, your right hand immediately draws the coin off the table as your left hand slaps down on the table, presumably with a coin under it. This time you leave your left hand palm down on the table.

Meanwhile, your right hand takes its coin below the top of the table, picks up the coin in your lap, and the right hand goes under the table.

With your left hand, perform a circular rubbing motion. Turn your hand over, showing that the coin is no longer on the table. Bring the two coins from under the table with your right hand and display them.

Examine the table at the point where you were slapping the coin down, saying:

"That hole must be bigger than I thought."

It's embarrassing to drop the coin into your lap and have it fall between your legs to the floor. To prevent this, stretch your legs forward under the table and cross your legs at the ankles. Then roll your legs inward, squeezing your thighs together. A woman wearing a skirt has a distinct advantage in performing this trick.

Coins and Cards

Every experienced coin magician performs a version of this trick. Coins mysteriously pass up through a table, appearing under a playing card or under a piece of cardboard.

Most versions call for considerable skill and sly moves, requiring countless hours of practice. This variation is very easy, yet completely deceptive.

Required are four pennies which look alike and two playing cards—preferably poker-size, because these cards are wider than "normal" cards. You can perform this trick on a bare table or on a table with a covering on which a coin will slide easily. The critical move involves sneakily sliding a coin, so a nubby tablecloth will make a proper presentation impossible. If need be, set a large magazine or a file folder on the table.

Lay out four pennies in a square. The pennies should be about six inches apart. Hold the two cards face

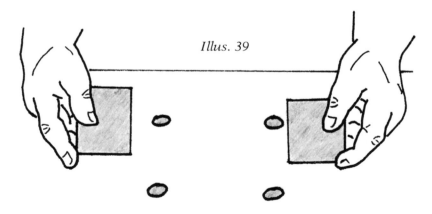

Illus. 39

down, one in each hand (Illus. 39). Set the card in your *right* hand on top of the upper-left penny, retaining your grip on the card. You explain:

"For this experiment to work, we must get the precisely correct magical combination. We can cover a coin with one card, or we can cover it with two."

Set the card in the left hand on top of the other card, retaining your grip on the card (Illus. 40).

Slide the card in your right hand to the right, covering the upper-right coin, still retaining your grip on the card.

"Cover two pennies separately . . ."

Set the card in your left hand on top of the other card, again keeping your grip.

". . . or cover one with two cards."

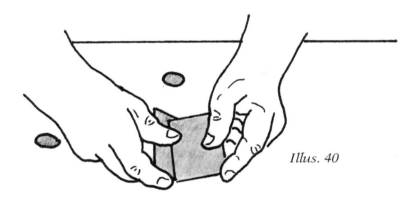

Illus. 40

Slide the card in your right hand down to cover the lower-right coin, keeping your grip, and say:

"Cover two pennies separately . . ."

As before, set the left-hand card on top, retaining your grip, and say:

". . . or cover one with two cards."

Slide the card in your *left* hand to the left, covering the lower-left coin. The back of your middle fingers of your left hand, at the knuckle below the fingernails, should be resting on the penny.

"Cover two pennies separately . . ."

Set the card in your right hand on top, keeping your grip on it.

". . . or cover one with two cards."

Now for the key move. Slide your left hand up to cover the upper-left penny with the card. Along with it, slide the penny which is resting under your fingers (Illus. 41). Let go of the card. Two pennies are now

Illus. 41

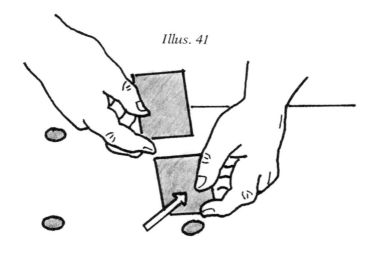

A coin is being slid forward under the card.

resting under it. As soon as the upward movement of the card in your left hand leaves enough room, drop the card in your right hand, presumably covering the lower-left coin.

As you perform the upward movement of the left hand, say:

"Cover two pennies separately . . ."

You have now dropped both cards.

"That's it!" you declare. "The right combination."

All of the above is down quite rapidly, without pause.

Casually draw back your left hand and let that hand fall into your lap. At the same time, pick up the upper-right coin in your right hand. Hold it up, and announce:

"Let's try this one first."

Bring the coin under the table and tap the underside of the table with your second finger. Try to tap with the end of the fingernail to provide a somewhat metallic sound. Later you'll be tapping *without* a coin, so this sound must be repeated each time.

As you bring your right hand back, toss the penny into your left hand, where it lies on the fingers. Without pausing, bring the right hand out. Reach towards the upper-left card with your palm up. The idea is to show that your hand is empty (without being too obvious). Lift the card off the two pennies.

"Good! It worked."

As you say this, bring the card back to your left hand, which takes it slightly below table level. Under the card, of course, you're holding a penny with your left fingers.

Immediately move your right hand to the two coins, and pick them up and hold them in the air. As you place the card and coin (that are in your left hand) down in the upper-left position, rattle the coins in your right hand, and say:

"Two pennies."

Your left hand now withdraws to the relaxed position on your lap. Your right hand drops the two coins onto the back of the card you just placed down.

The rattling of the coins in your right hand mis-directs the spectators' attention from your placement of the card with the coin underneath.

With your right hand, pick up the penny in the lower-right corner, and say:

"Now we'll try this one."

Take the coin under the table, tap, toss it into your left hand, and bring out your empty right hand. Move your right hand palm up to the card in the upper-left corner. Tilt the card so that the pennies on top slide off. Now move the card away, showing that another penny has passed through the table. As before, your right hand moves back and places the card in the left hand, which holds a penny underneath.

Promptly move your right hand forward, pick up the three pennies on the table, and hold them in the air. As you place the card and penny down in the upper-left position, rattle the coins, and say:

"Three pennies."

Drop the pennies on top of the card you just placed down.

The position of the objects on the table should be as follows: In the upper-left corner, you have a card with one penny under it and three pennies on top of it. In the lower-left corner is a card with no coin under it.

Here is the swindle. Place the cupped left hand a few inches below the table, directly behind the card in the lower-left corner. With fingers on top and thumb at the back, slide the card slightly off the table. As soon as the edge of the card clears the table, with your thumb lift the end of the card about 1". Perform a sweeping motion towards yourself, apparently sweeping the penny off the table into your cupped left hand. Close the left hand as though you were now holding the coin.

"And now this one," you say.

Simultaneously perform two actions. Bring your left hand under the table and tap the underside of the table with your second finger, and then turn the card in your right hand face up and toss it to the right of the other card. This will obscure your sneakiness.

Bring your left hand out and reach palm up towards the card in the upper-left corner. Tilt the card, sliding the three pennies off. Lift the card, showing that the last penny has penetrated the table. Turn the card face up and toss it on top of the other face-up card. Show both sides of your hands, and gather up your materials.

Since this is a fast trick, spectators are likely to be quite dazzled. You may well get a request to repeat it. Simply shake your head and say:

"No, I could never get exactly the right combination again."

To learn this trick, go through it slowly, omitting nothing. Every move has its purpose. Leave out one move and the trick may fail.

You'll know that you're ready to perform the trick publicly when you can go through it quickly and without pause. Performed rapidly, this trick has enormous impact as one coin after another passes through the table and under the card.

Practise your patter as you practise the movements.

This trick is an excellent example of the "one-ahead" principle, which is used in quite a few tricks. Such tricks work because the "dirty work" is done before the spectators are ready to look for it.

Classic Coins Through the Table

Here's a version of one of the most famous coin tricks of all. The effect is truly astonishing. Under the most impossible conditions, the performer seems to pass three coins through a solid table.

The key move requires precise timing; this will take considerable practice. But it will be worth it, for this trick can establish your reputation!

Place six quarters and one half-dollar on the table. Place the quarters in two parallel vertical rows of three each. The rows should be several inches apart. At the top of the row on the right, place the fifty-cent piece. From your viewpoint, the coins should be lined up to look like the drawing below.

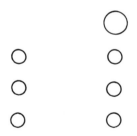

"We are using seven coins," you explain, "because seven is my lucky number. Sometimes."

You simultaneously pick up the two rows, the one on the left with the left hand, the one on the right with your right hand. Start at the top of each row and work towards you. With the right hand, pick up the fifty-cent piece first, and place it on top of the upper quarter. Both are placed on top of the second quarter. And all are placed on top of the near quarter. At the conclusion, the coins are held between your thumb and your fingers, your thumb against the fifty-cent piece. Raise the coins so that they're on edge, resting on the table.

Meanwhile, the left hand has picked up the row on the left, starting with the upper quarter. No attempt is made to pile the coins. At the end, they're held in a loose fist. Turn your hand over so that the back of your hand rests on the table.

Slide your right hand forward to the middle of the table. Tap the fifty-cent piece against the wood, and say:

"The table is very solid on top."

Move your right hand under the table. Set the pile of coins on your leg. Take the fifty-cent piece off the pile, reach under to the middle of the table, and tap the underside of the table with the coin. Say:

"And—surprise, surprise—it's also solid under here."

To cover the slight pause when you leave the quarters on your leg, you might laboriously move your body closer to the table, as though you were trying to reach further under the table; then do the tapping.

Immediately after tapping beneath the table, bring your right hand back to the table, holding your hand in a loose fist. Place your hand so that the back of the hand rests on the table. The hands should be separated by a hand's width plus a few inches (Illus. 42).

Roll your left hand clockwise, opening it and slapping its coins to the table. Immediately roll your hand back. Your hand is still open so that all can see that it is empty. Say:

"Three coins in this hand."

Turn your left hand over and gather up the three quarters with your fingers. The hand is back up. The coins are resting on the table, loosely held between the tips of your fingers and the heel of your palm.

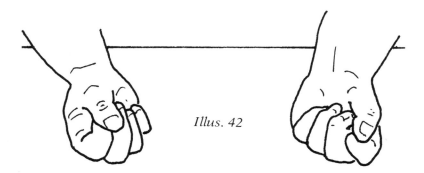

Illus. 42

Here's the trick move. Two things take place simultaneously: Your left hand lets go of its coins and then rolls counterclockwise in a loose fist. The right hand also rolls counterclockwise as it slaps the fifty-cent piece on top of the three quarters. Immediately roll your right hand back, still open, and say:

"And four coins in this hand."

Pick up the coins with your right hand, holding the coins in a loose fist. As you do so, say:

"A total of seven . . . perhaps my lucky number."

Bring your right hand under the table. Pick up the coins off your leg, adding them to the ones already in your right hand. As before, move your body closer to the table to cover the brief pause. Bring your right hand with its coins to the middle of the underside of the table.

Slide your left hand to the middle of the table. Turn your hand over and slap it palm down on the table. At the same time, shake your right hand so that the coins jingle. Turn over your left hand, showing that it's empty, and that there are no coins on the table. Bring your right hand from under the table, in a loose fist. Turn your hand over and spread the seven coins out on the table. Say:

"It worked! Seven *is* my lucky number."

One reason that this trick works so well is that fifty-cent piece in your right hand. After you've slapped the fifty-cent piece on top of the three quarters on the table, spectators make an assumption that you were holding a fifty-cent piece and three quarters in your right hand, and since there are three quarters and a fifty-cent piece on the table, these must be the same coins as you held in your right hand.

The basic move must be practised until you even fool yourself. To get the timing just right—rolling the left hand out of the way just as your right hand is slapping down the fifty-cent piece—practise at first *without* coins. When you do add the coins, the move will be much easier to perform.

Remember that you're *not* performing a trick move. Do not tense up. Some performers get anxious just before performing a move, and this nervousness serves as a virtual announcement that something tricky is coming. The idea is that you are just *showing* the coins held by each hand; try to treat it as casually as that.

Don't repeat this trick for the same audience. Consider the requests to repeat the trick as a form of applause. Take a bow and proceed to another trick.

In your patter, don't mention that you are going to try to pass coins through the table; there's no need to put the spectators on guard.

The real key to proper performance of this trick is confidence. If you practise until the moves are automatic, you will have that confidence.

· 6 ·

HAND-
KERCHIEF
TRICKS

Hanky-Panky _____

There are several methods of passing a coin through a handkerchief. This trick may be the best of the lot; coincidentally, it's also the easiest.

It is best to use a fifty-cent piece, although a quarter will do.

Display the coin in your left hand, first and second fingers in front, thumb behind (Illus. 43).

Illus. 43

With your right hand, drape a handkerchief over the coin. Approach the handkerchief from the top with the right hand, ostensibly to adjust the coin. Your fingers are in front and your thumb is behind. Actually, the right thumb digs a depression behind the coin, forming a fold which is held by the left thumb (Illus. 44). It's important that the fold be made at least ½" *below* the

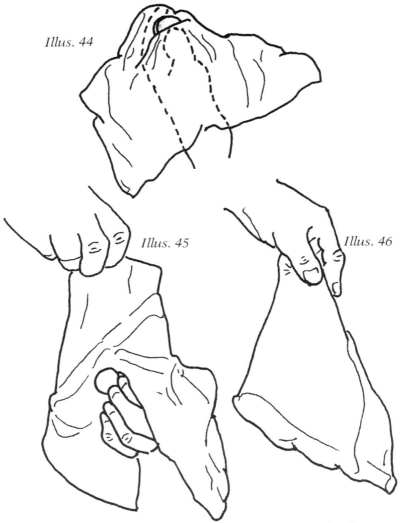

Illus. 44

Illus. 45

Illus. 46

coin. Lift up the front corner of the handkerchief just high enough to display the coin (Illus. 45).

Drop the corner, so that the handkerchief once more covers the coin. *Immediately*, turn your left hand down, dropping the back half of the handkerchief over the front half (Illus. 46). The spectators cannot see it, of course, but the coin is actually outside the handkerchief, at the rear.

Now comes the part that's often neglected. Raise your left hand so that it's parallel to the floor. Pass your right hand over the coin, folding the fabric around it. With your right fingers, pull slightly on the handkerchief, outlining the coin (Illus. 47). Twist the handkerchief around and around so that the coin is isolated.

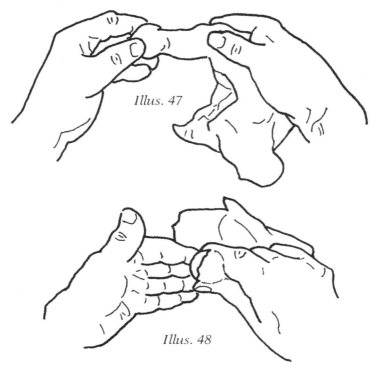

Illus. 47

Illus. 48

With your right fingers, very slowly squeeze the coin out and into the left hand (Illus. 48). It appears that you're squeezing the coin right through the fabric of the handkerchief.

This last touch makes the trick even more amazing. With your right first finger and your thumb, hold the handkerchief at the point where the coin emerged, letting the handkerchief unwind. Then, with both hands, very carefully spread the handkerchief so that everyone can see that there is no hole where the coin passed through.

The Magic Circle

A coin is placed in a handkerchief, which is held in the left hand. The coin mysteriously disappears. This is an excellent old trick, which would be enormously improved if you could show that the coin is not in your right hand, but you can't.

This method gets rid of the coin, enhancing the trick and also providing additional entertainment. For the trick to work, all spectators must be directly in front of you.

Hold your left hand palm up and drape a handkerchief over it. The hand should be at the center of the handkerchief. One corner of the handkerchief should rest on your wrist.

Place a fifty-cent piece in the center of the handkerchief so that you can grip the coin through the fabric with your left hand, fingers at the front and thumb at the back. About two-thirds of the coin should be showing (Illus. 49).

With your right hand, grasp the corner of the handkerchief which is resting on your wrist and bring it forward over the coin. As the handkerchief covers the coin, turn your left hand over so that your fingers point to the floor. Move your right hand away and point to the coin under the handkerchief, and say:

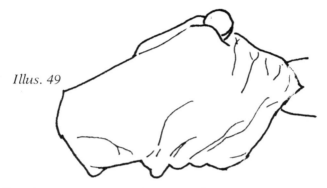

Illus. 49

"Did everyone see the coin?"

Reverse the motions just described, so that the fifty-cent piece is again on display. Move your left hand from side to side so that all may see the coin.

"A fifty-cent piece," you declare.

Again cover the coin as you did before the last step. But, as your right hand reaches its lowest position,

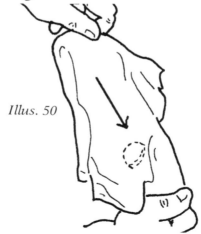

Illus. 50

release your grip on the coin, dropping it into your cupped right fingers (Illus. 50). As before, point to the presumed coin under the handkerchief, raising the handkerchief to arm's length above your head. The coin, of course, is held by the cupped second, third, and fourth fingers of your right hand. Casually let your right hand drop to your side.

As you raise the handkerchief above your head, start turning around clockwise. With little shuffles of the feet, turn in a complete circle, yet stay in the same place. Your left hand continues to hold the handkerchief high above your head. Throughout the turn, you will talk, saying something like this:

"Have you ever heard of the magic circle? Well, before your very eyes I am making a magic circle right now. There is no extra charge for this feat. I'm happy to do it for you. Who knows? Maybe someday you'll learn to make a magic circle of your own."

By this time, you should be facing the front again. While making your "magic circle," you did something extremely sneaky. When your left side was towards the audience, you dropped the coin into your right trouser pocket. Or, if that pocket wasn't available, you might have tucked it under the top of your trousers or your skirt.

You're still holding the handkerchief (and supposedly, the coin) at arm's length above your head. Reach up with your right hand and take a corner of the handkerchief between your first and second fingers. Let go with the left hand and let the handkerchief fall, held only at the corner by the right fingers. This is a very showy climax.

You're holding one corner of the handkerchief between two fingers of your right hand. Switch the grip, so that you're holding it between your thumb and first finger. Take an adjacent corner between the thumb

and first finger of your left hand and spread the handkerchief between the hands, palms to the audience.
Reverse the position of your hands, showing the other
side of the handkerchief. Give the handkerchief to your
audience for them to examine and show both sides of
both hands.

Say, "Thank goodness the magic circle worked!"

While you make your magic circle, all attention is on
the handkerchief you are holding aloft. This misdirection of the audience's attention is perfect for ditching
the coin.

Not a Knot

This handkerchief trick is much easier to perform than
it is to describe. Follow along with a handkerchief and
pay close attention to the illustrations. For clarity, the
handkerchief is shown quite a bit thinner than it actually is.

Place the handkerchief so that you're holding it
about 3″ below a corner between the first and second
fingers of your left hand, the rest of the handkerchief
hanging down. Hold the cloth about 3″ down from the
tip so that the "knot" will be fairly near the middle of
the handkerchief.

Fold in your third and fourth fingers, pressing
against the handkerchief; then with the right hand,
take the opposite corner and place it in the fork of your
thumb (Illus. 51).

Bend in your left second finger so that it presses
against the handkerchief at the point shown in Illus.
52. With your right hand, reach *through* the loop. With
your thumb and first and second fingers, grasp the end
indicated by the arrow shown in Illus. 52.

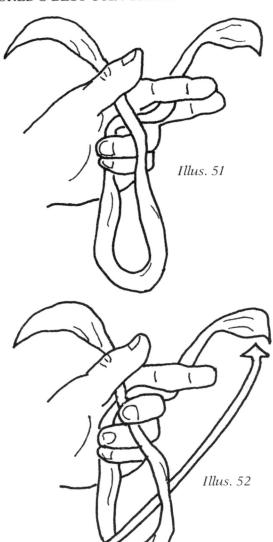

Illus. 51

Illus. 52

Now perform two actions simultaneously: First, draw your right hand back through the loop it just entered, bringing with it the end it's holding. Second, turn your left hand clockwise about one half-turn. Almost automatically, the *back* of your left second finger presses against the handkerchief, forming a loop as you pull on the end (Illus. 53). Make sure that the loop is on the side away from the spectators. Illus. 54 shows the loop being tightened as you continue to pull down on the end with your right hand.

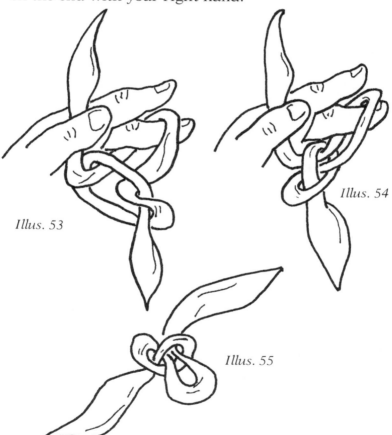

Illus. 53

Illus. 54

Illus. 55

Pull down the end very rapidly, virtually *jerking* it, so that the handkerchief forms a knot. Actually, it's a slipknot, for you're still holding a loop with your left second finger. Illus. 55 shows how the "knot" looks after you've taken away your left second finger.

Give the end another quick jerk, and then remove your finger from the loop and slide your left hand to the top of the handkerchief, where your left hand holds that end. The other end is held in your right hand.

Holding the handkerchief horizontally between your hands, approach a spectator. Ask him to blow on the knot. When he does so, pull the ends, popping the knot out.

It takes only a few seconds to tie the fake knot. The key, as with so many tricks, is smoothness. Practise until the moves become second nature to you; it won't take long.

Loose Ends

In this trick, you'll tie the two ends of the handkerchief together. A spectator will tighten the knot. Nevertheless, you'll cause the knot to vanish.

The problem is to look as though you're actually tying the ends of the handkerchief together in a normal fashion. First, try the regular way of knotting the ends.

Hold one end of the handkerchief in each hand. Cross the ends. Bring one end through the loop formed. Tie the two ends into a square knot.

Now try the trick method. Again, hold one end of the handkerchief in each hand, and then cross the ends (Illus. 56). Shift your grip so that your left hand holds end "A," and your right hand holds end "B." As you speak to your audience, casually wind end "A" around end "B," and again shift your grip so that your left hand now holds end "B" and your right hand holds end "A." Illus. 57 shows how the handkerchief looks now.

The fingers of both hands prevent spectators from seeing the actual situation.

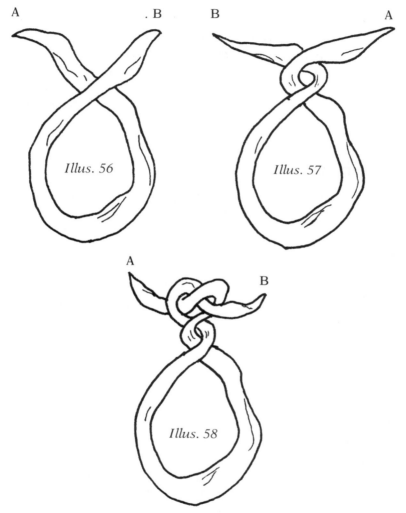

Illus. 56

Illus. 57

Illus. 58

Now, with your right hand shielding the portion where the handkerchief crosses, tie the ends in a square knot. Pull the ends fairly tight (Illus. 58).

Hold the handkerchief in your right hand just below the knot in the cloth, concealing the portion of cloth where the handkerchief crosses. Approach a spectator and ask him to pull the ends tight. Make sure that you hold on tight as the spectator pulls.

Hold the handkerchief on each side of the "knot," pushing in slightly to make sure that the "knot" doesn't unwind prematurely. Ask the spectator to blow on the knot. When he does so, pull with both of your hands, and, of course, the knot will disappear.

S-T-R-E-T-C-H

This unusual and amusing stunt makes it seem that you actually stretch a cloth handkerchief.

Extend a handkerchief between your hands at chest level, holding it about 2″ in from each end (Illus. 59).

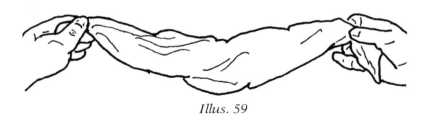

Illus. 59

Say:

"Have you noticed that new stretch material they're putting in handkerchiefs these days? Just watch."

Twirl the handkerchief in one tight circle, letting a minute amount of the fabric slide through the fingers of both of your hands. Do this again, and again, and again. In all, you will do it ten to fifteen times, until you're barely hanging on to the ends with the tips of your fingers and thumb.

Actually, you will have "stretched" the handkerchief only about 4". Each twirl, however, has wound the handkerchief tighter and made it thinner, so that the illusion is created that the handkerchief has gotten much longer.

At the conclusion, display the handkerchief between your hands for a moment or two, saying, "See?" Let loose of one end, shake the handkerchief, bunch it up, and (before putting it away) hold it up, and say:

"Just as well. I feel a cold coming on. I can use all the handkerchief I can get."

Silly!

This is not a trick, but it's an entertaining stunt you can perform for children.

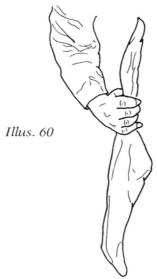

Illus. 60

Holding a handkerchief in your right hand, grab a corner with your left hand and pull up so that about 6" stand straight up in the air (Illus. 60). Note that your right fingers are in front of the handkerchief and your thumb is behind.

Stroke the handkerchief up with the left fingers several times, straightening it, and say:

"This is a magic handkerchief. You have probably noticed that one person here is very, very silly. Now when I wave my hand over the handkerchief and say the magic word . . . which is 'silly' . . . the handkerchief will *point* to the person who . . ."

As you say "point," press your right thumb against your right first finger through the handkerchief. The spire you have formed with the handkerchief will fall towards you, pointing at you.

Stop talking as you notice what's happened. Quickly straighten out the spire, stroking the handkerchief upward as before.

"As I was saying, someone here is extremely silly. This magic handkerchief will *point* to that person when I . . ."

Once more you press your thumb against your first finger, and the handkerchief will point at you. This time, and succeeding times, you should continue talking for a bit. Children find it quite funny that you're unaware that the handkerchief is pointing at you.

You notice that the handkerchief is pointing at you. Now you are getting a bit irritated as you repeat the entire business. Children will find each repetition increasingly amusing. Four or five repetitions should be enough. Finally, say:

"You know something? This handkerchief is really *dumb*!"

Put the handkerchief away, and proceed with something else.

· 7 ·

STUNTS

A stunt is a feat displaying unusual strength, skill, or daring.

Rolling a Coin

Few things are as impressive to spectators as the ability to roll a coin over the back of your fingers. It is, in fact, fairly difficult, requiring considerable practice. But, you can learn it if you have determination and a little patience. And once you master the stunt, you'll be able to use it forever.

It's best to practise over a bed or a couch, or sitting at a table. It gets terribly tiresome picking the coin up off the floor. The best coin to use is a half-dollar, although a quarter will do.

Most of those who attempt the stunt try to roll the coin well down on the fingers. Actually, the coin is

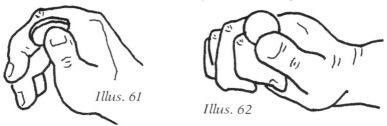

Illus. 61

Illus. 62

rolled just below the knuckles, where your fingers begin.

The coin is balanced on your right thumb (Illus. 61). Note that your hand is slightly cupped. The coin is brought next to your first finger, where the coin is lightly pinched between your thumb and first finger (Illus. 62).

Your thumb pushes the coin up until it drops on the back of your first finger (Illus. 63). Note that your other fingers are raised, preparatory to doing their job.

Your second finger is lowered, clipping the end of the coin and tilting the coin upwards (Illus. 64). As your

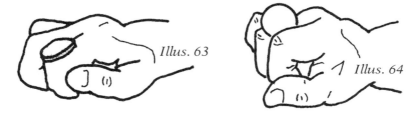

Illus. 63

Illus. 64

first finger is raised, the coin falls on the back of your second finger. Your third and fourth fingers are raised.

Your third finger clips the edge of the coin, and then lowers, turning the coin over (Illus. 65).

Now comes the hard part. The coin rests on the back of your third finger. Lift your fourth finger quite high,

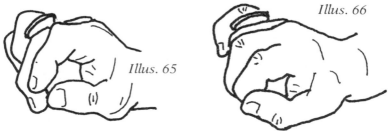

Illus. 66

Illus. 65

grasping the coin. Slide your third finger up as you lower your fourth finger, letting the coin slide partly through (Illus. 66).

Bring your thumb under your hand and let the half-dollar rest on your thumb (Illus. 67). The thumb brings the coin back, and you're ready to roll the coin again. For best effect, do it several times.

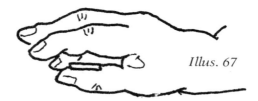

Illus. 67

Once you know the moves, strive for a smooth, rolling effect. It works best when you don't watch your hand. This is particularly true when you haven't done this trick for a while. Just let your reflexes take over.

Using Your Head

Choose a person to assist you and proceed to cause a coin to vanish. Everyone knows how you did it, *except* your assistant. This generates considerable amusement. But then, in a humorous climax, you also let your assistant in on the secret.

Select as your assistant a good sport. Have him stand facing you, both of you with your sides to the audience.

Display a quarter or a fifty-cent piece. Say to your assistant:

"We're going to perform a little experiment to test your reflexes. On the count of three, I will place the coin in your hand, and you should close your hand and grab the coin. But you'll have to be fast. So hold out your hand palm up, please. Ready?"

Hold the coin between your thumb and fingers. The coin should be near the tips of the fingers, but it shouldn't extend beyond them. You're now going to rapidly swing your arm up so that your hand is about 2″ above your head. Immediately swing your arm down again and lightly touch the coin to the palm of the spectator's hand. As you near the hand, say, "One!"

Repeat the motions, saying, "Two!" Repeat the motions, saying, "Three!" Your assistant should grab the coin. But whether he does or not, leave the coin in his palm and quickly withdraw your hand. Casually show that your hand is empty and ask your assistant, "Did you get it?" Of course he did. Compliment him on his reflexes. Take the coin back, saying, "Let's try it again."

Repeat the actions through a count of one and two. As your hand comes above your head the third time, place the coin right on top of your head. Instantly bring your arm down as before, saying, "Three!" As before, quickly withdraw your hand. Ask, "Did you get it?" Of course he didn't, although he may think he did. Have him open his hand. Display both of your empty hands. Say, "Magic." The audience should be amused, and your assistant should be quite puzzled.

Pause for a bit, basking in the glory of your achievement. Then say, "Thank you, thank you," and take a little bow, letting the coin fall off your head to the floor. Snap your fingers in mock disgust.

"Doggone it! I always forget."

When you swing the coin above your head and down to your assistant's hand, always keep the back of your hand towards your assistant.

Rarely, an assistant (particularly a tall one) will know what you've done. Since you're performing more of a stunt than a magic trick, this discovery doesn't diminish the fun. If this happens to you, feign great chagrin and confess that your helper is too smart for you. Then pretend to take the coin in one hand, performing one of the vanishes. Extend the hand presumably containing the coin to your assistant, saying, "Here, you keep the money." Invariably the spectator reaches to take the coin, and you show the hand empty. "Those are the breaks," you say, and then you cause the coin to reappear from somewhere.

Heads Up

Use a fifty-cent piece or a quarter for this stunt. A tricky movement is required, but you should master it after five or ten minutes of practice.

The idea is to convince spectators that you have a double-headed coin.

Hold the coin, the head side up, in the palm of your right hand, slightly to the left of the middle of your palm.

Say, "Have you ever seen a two-headed coin?"

Display the coin so that all can see it. Hold both hands palms up, your left hand about 6″ from your right hand and about 2″ lower than your right hand (Ilus. 68).

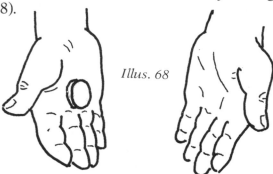

Illus. 68

Jerk your right hand quickly to the left, letting the coin slide off your right palm and onto your left palm.

Obviously, it falls face up (Illus. 69). In the same motion, slap your right hand palm down on your left palm (Illus. 70). This move is done quite rapidly. The illusion

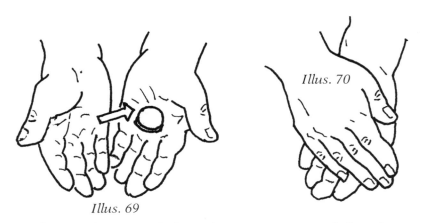

Illus. 70

Illus. 69

is that you've turned the coin over onto your left palm. Lift up your right hand to show that, evidently, the other side of the coin is also a head.

Using the same move, return the coin to your right hand. Show the coin.

Return the coin to your left hand, and then back to your right. You've adequately demonstrated that you have a two-headed coin. You should have a strong ending. Say:

"Many people have offered me a dollar for this fabulous two-headed coin."

Address one of the spectators:

"Would you be willing to pay a dollar for this?"

As you say this, place the coin in your left hand so that the tail side is up. Since you don't want anyone to see the tail side, use the legitimate version of the *Easy Vanish* move (page 13). Hold the coin between thumb and fingers in your right hand, and the coin will naturally turn over as you place it in the palm of your left hand. Close your left fingers over the coin as you withdraw your right hand.

If the spectator says that he would be willing to pay a dollar, open your left hand, saying, "Bad choice." Display the coin on your left palm, showing the tail side. Then lift the coin up and show both sides.

If the spectator says that he wouldn't be willing to pay a dollar, say, "Good thinking," and display the coin as above.

Easy Call

To perform this stunt, you must learn a tricky move. The move isn't difficult, however, and the effort will be well rewarded.

Use a half-dollar, although a quarter will do. Flip the coin about 18″ into the air with your right thumb, catch the coin, and then slap the coin onto your left wrist. Illus. 71 shows how to hold the coin when you're about to flip it.

Illus. 71

As you flip the coin and slap it onto your wrist a few times, say:

"Wouldn't it be wonderful if you could always tell the way the coin would end up?"

You then call heads or tails, as you flip the coin. Catch the coin, slap it onto your wrist, and, sure enough, you're right.

Actually, you do not *flip* the coin, although it certainly looks like it. You look at the coin lying in your hand. Suppose that the head side is up. You'll catch it the same way. When you slap the coin onto your wrist, the coin will be turned over. So, as you perform the pseudo-flipping action, you call tails.

Here's the trick move. Hold the coin in your hand as before, but with a slight variation. Your thumb is held back from the coin, and your first finger is above the tip of the coin (Illus. 72). Don't *flip* the coin into the air,

Illus. 72

but propel it upwards in a quick hand movement resembling the regular flipping motion. As you propel the coin upwards, let the side of the coin tick against your first finger. This will give the coin a wobbling motion which looks very much like a regular spin. Naturally, the coin never actually turns over; it returns to your hand with the same side up as when you tossed it.

This move is easy enough to practise, and it shouldn't take you long to get the knack.

Stuck with a Penny

Get a good sport to assist you. Take a penny at the edges and hold it up to your forehead, tail side towards your forehead. Rub it into your forehead, turning the coin in place in a slight circular fashion. The coin will adhere to your forehead. Now say:

"It's easy enough to take the penny away when you use your hands, but otherwise it can be very difficult."

Wrinkle your face up, trying to dislodge the penny. Assume that you aren't successful. Take the penny from your forehead and say to your assistant:

"I wonder if *you* could do it. Okay?"

Again holding the coin at the edges, rub it into your assistant's forehead, *but take the coin away*, dropping your hand to your side. Say:

"Without using your hands, give it a try."

The audience should derive considerable amusement from your assistant's facial contortions as he tries to dislodge the coin.

After he tries for a while, casually begin flipping the penny and catching it. Eventually, he should get the idea and hold his hand to his forehead.

"Good heavens," you might say. "You made it disappear."

Occasionally, your assistant will notice immediately that you did not leave the penny on his forehead. You might say:

"You're right. To tell you the truth, I just didn't trust you with it."

It was once believed that the penny had to be moistened or it wouldn't adhere to the forehead, but this is not true.

Flip-Flop

You may perform this trick using either five half-dollars or five quarters. Half-dollars are better because they're easier for spectators to see. Not many people carry half-dollars, however, so if you're going to borrow the coins, use quarters.

Place the five coins on your left hand so that they overlap. Heads and tails should alternate. Say,

"Heads and tails intermixed. Let's see what we can do about that."

Meticulously push the coins into a stack with your right fingers and thumb. Hold the coins at the ends of your fingers and thumb as you lift the coins a few inches above your left hand (Illus. 73).

Illus. 73

You're now going to drop the coins one at a time onto your left palm. Assume for a moment that the coins are heads up, tails up, heads up, tails up, heads up. When you drop the first one, you will release pressure from both fingers and thumb simultaneously; the coin will fall directly into your left hand, still heads up. With the second coin, however, you will release only the thumb. This will cause the coin to pivot off the fingers and turn over, also landing heads up. The third coin is dropped regularly, the fourth caused to turn over, and the last dropped regularly.

Show that all the coins are now heads up. The stunt may be repeated.

It isn't easy learning how to drop the coins properly. First, you'll have to determine the correct distance separating your left and right hands. Second, you must figure out how you lessen the thumb pressure so that the coin will pivot off your right fingers and turn over; you must develop a certain "touch." The solution is practice!

· 8 ·

PENNIES GALORE

A rich variety of effects is available when performing with a deck of cards. Unfortunately, there's a limited number of coin effects. Granted, any number of methods may be used to accomplish an effect, but an audience does not necessarily appreciate your versatility. A coin trick generally takes less time to perform than a card trick. After performing coin tricks for ten minutes or so, you'll probably have done every possible effect. Unless, of course, you have thrown in a few extraordinary tricks requiring no sleight of hand—tricks such as the ones in this chapter.

To Coin a Phrase

The person doing coin tricks shouldn't confine himself to sleight-of-hand effects. In a Shakespearean play, comedy heightens tragedy and vice versa. In coin magic, sleight-of-hand effects can be mixed with "non-sleight" tricks, enhancing both. The following trick was originally a card trick.

Say, "I have developed the ability to estimate perfectly the number of coins a person takes. I do this in a single glance."

Engage the services of a friendly spectator. Tell him:

"Grab some pennies, and I'll demonstrate."

The spectator grabs several pennies.

"Hide them," you say. "And I'll take some."

You grab a handful of pennies.

"Now I'll turn my back. You count your pennies, and I'll count mine."

You both do so. When you turn back, you say:

"I have the same number of pennies you have, three left over, and enough more to make your pennies total twelve."

Repeat the statement.

Let's suppose that the spectator took eight pennies.

Say, "Let's count them together."

He counts his in front of him, as you count yours separately. The coins need not be counted one on top of the other.

As the two of you count, you say aloud:

"One, two, three, four, five, six, seven, eight."

When finished, you say:

"I said, 'Three left over.' "

Count off three pennies to one side.

"And I said, 'Enough left over to make your pennies total twelve.' You have eight there."

Count from your hand onto his pile.

"Nine, ten, eleven, twelve."

You are out of pennies. You are exactly right. You had the same number he had, three left over, and enough more to make his pennies total twelve.

Basically, you have baffled the spectators with a semantic trick. All you did was to make sure that you had several more pennies than the spectator did.

When you counted your pennies, you discovered that you had fifteen. You mentally subtracted three (for the number left over), and came up with the number twelve. You then told the spectator that you had the same number, three left over, and enough more to make his pennies total twelve. In effect, you told him that you counted your pennies and that you had fifteen; you merely stated it in a subtle way.

Note that at the end you count the pennies onto the spectator's stack. This is the touch that makes the trick work. Somehow, it keeps the victim from realizing that you are *actually* saying:

"I have twelve pennies and three left over."

Once more, all you have to do is to make sure that you have a larger number of pennies than the spectator has. Next, count the pennies, subtract a suitable small number (two, three, or four) for misdirection, and then make your statement.

Let's try one more example. Suppose the spectator grabs a dozen or so pennies. When you count your pennies, you discover you have nineteen. You might say:

"I have the same number of pennies as you have, two left over, and enough more to make your pennies total seventeen."

We'll say the spectator has ten coins. Count aloud as you each count your pennies into separate piles. Set two aside—"two left over."

Then say, "You have ten there."

Count the rest of yours onto his pile, starting with eleven. And, of course, you run out of pennies when you count out the seventeenth.

The Farmer's Will

This is more of a puzzle than it is a trick, but the climax

is quite surprising, and the story still entertains.

You say:

"An old farmer had two things he valued: his mules and his sons. He had seventeen mules and three sons. These pennies will stand for the mules." Count seventeen pennies onto the table. Ask a spectator to check the count.

Say:

"When the farmer died, he left his seventeen mules to his sons. He left one-half to his oldest son, one-third to his second oldest son, and one-ninth to his youngest son. Now the sons didn't know much about math . . . or anything else, for that matter. But they *were* smart enough to consult a lawyer. The lawyer had a high school education, so he knew that he couldn't divide up seventeen mules that way. So the lawyer cheerfully donated one mule of his own."

Add another penny to the group on the table.

"At the price he was charging the sons, he could afford it."

Gesture towards the coins on the table.

"So now there were eighteen mules. He gave one-half to the oldest son. That's nine mules."

Count out nine pennies and push them into a separate pile.

"He gave one-third to the second oldest son. That's six mules."

Count out six pennies and push them into a separate pile.

"And he gave one-ninth to the youngest son. That's two mules."

Count out two pennies and push them into a separate pile.

One penny remains in the middle of the table. Point to it, saying:

"And the laywer was amazed to find that he got his mule back."

The trick is based on the fact that the farmer did not actually leave all his mules to his sons; he left only 17/18 of them. He left 1/2, 1/3, and 1/9; in other words, 9/18, 6/18, and 2/18. 9, 6, and 2 add up to 17; thus, 17/18.

Too Many Pennies

In its original version, this was a game at which the spectator seldom (if ever) won. In this version of the trick, the spectator *never* wins, and the presentation provides considerable amusement.

Suppose that you have a fairly large number of pennies on the table. Count out 13 and push the rest aside.

"We'll use 13 pennies," you say.

"As you know, some people consider 13 an unlucky number. So I need a volunteer who's not superstitious."

Josh with the group until you get a volunteer.

Address your helper:

"I challenge you to a game of Skunk. We have 13 pennies here. You can take one coin or two coins. Then I take one or two coins. We keep on until only one is left. Whoever has to take the last one is a Skunk. You start this time. I'll start next time. And let's go as fast as we can. Ready, set, go!"

The spectator is skunked no matter what. Let us say the spectator takes two pennies; you take one. If he takes one, you take two. You continue doing this until there is one coin left on the table, and it's the volunteer's turn.

"Too bad," you say. "You were skunked."

Clearly, the spectator can perform the same feat, if you're the first one to choose and *if* you play with the same number of coins. So let's change the number of coins.

Gather the 13 pennies into a group.

"Too many pennies for you," you say.

"How many do you want to throw out—one or two?"

Set aside one or two pennies, depending on his choice.

"Now it's my turn to start first," you say.

If he chose to set aside one penny, take two. If he chose two, take one. This means that he will be choosing from 10 pennies, and he can't win. You continue to take two when he takes one, and one when he takes two. Again he ends up with the last coin.

"Skunked again," you declare sorrowfully, gathering the coins again.

"You know why? Too many pennies!" you say.

Casually, set aside one or two pennies, whichever will reduce the total number to ten.

"That should be better. Go ahead. Take one or two."

It doesn't matter what the volunteer does. When you follow the same procedure as before, he can't win when he begins choosing from seven pennies.

"Skunked again," you say, collecting the seven pennies.

"You know why? Too many pennies. How many should we throw out—one or two?"

Set aside the number he indicates. It's your turn first. If he chose to set aside two, take one; if he chose one, take two. He has to choose from four and he can't win.

"Skunked again. You know why?"

He may answer, "Too many pennies."

Regardless, you say, "No, no, the problem is—*not enough pennies!*" Push all the pennies back into the center and say:

"We'll change the rules. You get the first turn, and you can take as many pennies as you want."

It shouldn't take him long to figure out that his best bet is taking all the pennies but one.

"I'm skunked!" you declare. "Doggone it, I was hoping you wouldn't think of that."

A Western Tale

Most people enjoy a trick with a story to go along with it. This trick, requiring no sleight of hand, is a good change of pace from snappy coin disappearances and reappearances.

You need seven pennies and one quarter. No penny should look markedly different from the others. Lay out five of the pennies on a table (or the floor, for that matter), like this:

Set the quarter off to the right side, and set the two remaining pennies near it.

"I'd like to tell you a little Western story," you say, "using these coins for markers. The five pennies I've laid out here are prize cattle, gathered in a corral. The quarter over there is big Lenny, the rancher who owns the cattle. He's in the ranch house."

Indicate the two pennies you set aside, saying:

"And these are two range tramps."

Point to one of the pennies.

"One evening this range tramp arrived at the ranch and asked Lenny to put him up for the night. Lenny said, 'All right. You can stay in one of the barns. But don't get any funny ideas about rustling my cattle, or I'll blow your head off.' So the tramp went into the barn."

Open your right hand.

"This is the barn."

Pick up the penny and hold it in your closed right hand.

"Coincidentaly, another range tramp rode in and asked the rancher if he could stay the night. Lenny said, 'Well, I already got a tramp sleeping in my good barn. You can stay in the other one. But don't get any funny ideas about rustling my cattle, or I'll blow you to pieces.' So this tramp went into the other barn."

Open your left hand.

"This is the other barn."

Pick up the penny and hold it in your closed left hand.

"But, of course, the tramps decided to steal the cattle and go off with them early in the morning. So they took them one by one."

Deliberately take a penny in your *right hand*. Then take one with your left hand. Continue alternating until all the pennies are in your hands. As you take the pennies, each hand should be in a fist, with the palm down.

Reach over with your right hand and move the quarter a bit closer to where the pennies had been originally laid out.

"Lenny may have looked dumb, but he was suspicious of those tramps, so he decided to go outside and have a look. Of course, the tramps heard him stomping around inside the ranch house, so they quickly returned the cattle to the corral."

Return the pennies to their original position, first one from your *left hand*, then one from the right, and continue alternating until all are returned. You now have two pennies in your right hand.

Raise both fists as you say:

"And, of course, the two sneaky tramps remained in the barns."

This is quite important, for it creates the impression that a coin is in each hand.

Edge the quarter near the pennies with your right hand.

"Lenny saw that the cattle were all right, so he returned to the ranch house."

Move the quarter back to its original position.

"Naturally, the greedy tramps stole the cattle again."

As before, alternate hands as you take the pennies, starting with your *right hand*.

"But Lenny was still suspicious. He grabbed his rifle and tiptoed out to the corral."

Move the quarter to where the pennies had been laid out.

"Lenny was pretty quick on the uptake. He noticed right away that the cattle were missing. So he decided to check out the barns. Only one way could those tramps save their lives: if they were together in one barn, and the cattle were together in the other. And sure enough, in *this* barn . . ."

Open your left hand.

". . . were the two tramps. And in the other barn . . ."

Open your right hand.

". . . were the five cattle."

Shake your head.

"I'll be darned if I know how those tramps did it."

The trick is automatic; just follow the directions. Remember to take pennies with your *right hand* first both times. When you put them back, start with your *left hand*.

This is a perfect choice after you have performed a number of sleight-of-hand tricks. Spectators tend to deceive themselves by watching for sleight of hand. Lenny, of course, is merely window dressing. Obviously, the trick should be done only once; a repetition risks discovery.

Pennies and Dimes

Often presented as a puzzle, this is an excellent quick trick.

You need ten pennies and ten dimes. Lay them out as in Illus. 74. The coins should be very close to one another, almost touching.

Say, "Here we have pennies and dimes intermixed, as you can see."

Give everyone a chance to look.

Take a good-size magazine in your left hand and rest an edge of the magazine on the table in front of the coins. Lean the magazine back so that the spectators can't see precisely what you're doing. With the first and second fingers of your right hand, slide the top two dimes up. Without changing the distance between them, slide the two dimes around the other coins to below the bottom two pennies (Illus. 75). Push the two

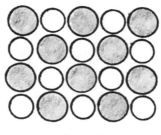

Illus. 74

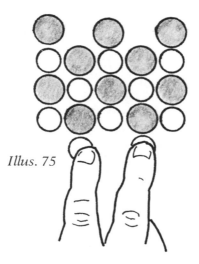

Illus. 75

dimes against these pennies so that the second and fourth columns of coins move up one coin (Illus. 76).

To confuse things, move your right hand in a rapid circular motion above the coins several times. Move the magazine aside.

"Now the coins are in perfect rows," you say.

Holding your first finger about 1" above the coins, run your finger across each horizontal row in turn, starting with the top row. As you do so, say:

"Pennies, dimes, pennies, dimes."

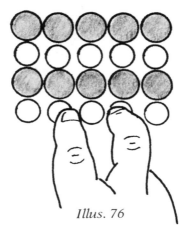

Illus. 76

Despite the shielding magazine, some spectators may see what you're doing, but it doesn't matter. They are unlikely to catch the exact move, and, even if they do get the right idea, they're unlikely to be able to duplicate the trick. Regardless, the trick is quickly done, and you immediately proceed to another. Naturally, don't repeat the trick.

· 9 ·

MENTAL MAGIC WITH COINS

When you perform a trick where you purport to be using telepathy, you should create the impression that you are actually trying to use your extrasensory powers. Concentrate, hold your hand to your forehead, receive your telepathic message gradually. Good acting heightens the trick's effectiveness and increases the fun.

Heads or Tails (1)

Through your mystical powers, you are able to divine whether a spectator has chosen heads or tails. You may repeat this several times.

The lengthy explanation may make the trick seem complicated. Actually, it's quite simple.

You may perform this with any coin denomination, and with any number of coins. Try to use seven to twelve quarters; it's easy to tell a head from a tail, and this is essential.

In this example, assume that you have ten quarters on the table. Count the number of heads showing, noting whether the number is odd or even. You notice that five heads are showing, so you say to yourself, "Odd."

Ask a spectator to assist you. Say:

"While my back is turned, I want you to turn over a coin. When you do, say, 'Turn.' You may do this as often as you wish. And you may do it with the same coin as often as you wish. Just remember to say, 'Turn' every time you turn a coin over. Tell me when you're done."

Turn your back to the spectator, and ask him to begin.

You noted an *odd* number of heads, so when the spectator says, "Turn," say to yourself, "Even." When again he says, "Turn," say to yourself, "Odd." Continue alternating like this until he says that he's done. You need only remember the last thing you said to yourself, "Odd" or "Even." In this instance, say that you are remembering "Odd."

Say, "Please slide a coin away from the rest and hide it under your hand."

When the spectator is ready, turn around. Study the hand under which the coin is hidden, stare into space, glance casually at the coins on the table. All the while, get a count of the number of heads now showing. Again, you note whether the number is odd or even.

You are remembering "Odd." If the number is odd, it is *the same* as the word you have in your mind. If the number is even, it is *different* from the number you have in your mind. Is the coin under the spectator's hand heads up or tails up? Easy. Just remember this: *different:* head; *the same:* tail.

Suppose you just noted that an odd number of heads is showing. You are remembering "Odd." They are the same. Therefore, think of *the same: tail*. The coin under the spectator's hand is tails up. Through extensive concentration, reveal this.

Here's another example. You count the number of coins that are heads up on the table, noting that the number is even. Turn your back. The first time the spectator turns a coin and says, "Turn," you say to yourself, "Odd." Next time, you say, "Even." Next time, "Odd." And so on. When the spectator says that he's done, you remember the last word. In this example, "Even." Your assistant hides a coin under his hand. You turn back and count the number of coins that have heads showing. In this instance, the number is odd. You are remembering "Even." They are *different*. You think, *"Different: head."* The coin under the spectator's hand is heads up.

The trick may be repeated several times. You may want to perform the basic trick a few times, and then try this variation. Instead of having your assistant slide one coin in front of him and conceal it under his hand, have him hide *two* coins. Count the heads, as before. If the number gives you a result that is *different*, your assistant has a head and a tail under his hand. If the number gives you a result that is *the same*, the spectator has either two heads or two tails under his hand.

It always goes over well when you tell your assistant that he has a head and a tail under his hand. But it is less effective when you must tell your assistant that both coins under his hand are the same. Instead of doing this, say:

"I just can't get it. The two coins are just too much for me. Would you push one out here."

Note what it is when he pushes it out; the other coin is the same. Concentrate, and then tell him what he's still concealing under his hand.

It doesn't matter how many coins you use in this trick. Clearly, the fewer you use, the faster you will be able to determine whether the number of heads is odd or even. Don't use fewer than seven coins, however. Another advantage to using seven coins is that you can talk about the mystical properties of seven, or of how seven has always been your lucky number.

Heads or Tails (2)

Here's a simpler version of the preceding trick. Both versions are quite effective, so you may decide to use one or the other. You may prefer to do them both. After doing the first version a few times, say:

"Let's make it more difficult. This time don't tell me when you turn the coins over."

You have a number of coins on the table; the number is irrelevant. You might prefer to use quarters because it's easier to tell heads from tails. Count the number of heads and remember whether the number is odd or even. Suppose that the number of heads is odd. All you need to remember is *odd*.

Say to your assistant:

"I would like you to turn over two coins at a time. Do this as many times as you wish. You may turn over any two, including one or both of the ones you just turned over. Don't let me hear you turn them over, and certainly don't tell me when you're turning them over. When you are done turning the coins over, slide one under your hand. I'm going to put my hands over my ears, so tap me on the back when you're all done."

Turn away and put your hands over your ears. When you turn around after the spectator taps you on the back, count the heads on the coins, noting whether the number is odd or even. Suppose that the number is odd. Since you're remembering *odd*, the two are *the same*. As with the first version, you think,

"The same: *tail*."

Your assistant will reveal a tail when he lifts up his hand.

In this example, suppose that when you turn around, the number of heads on the table is even. This is *different* from odd. You think,

"Different: *head*."

In other words, you use precisely the same code as in the first version of this trick. The only difference is that in this variation, you don't keep track of the number of turns the spectator makes.

Don't neglect to gradually name heads or tails as you get "mental vibrations" from your assistant.

Row, Row

This trick can be performed with coins, poker chips, or other small objects. Let's assume you're working with pennies. There should be at least 20 to 25 pennies on the table.

Get a volunteer and say:

"Let's try an experiment in telepathy. While my back is turned, I'd like you to make two rows of pennies. The top row should have one more penny than the bottom row."

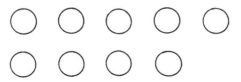

Show him what you mean by setting up two rows of pennies, five in the top row and four in the bottom row. The rows should look like the drawing at the bottom of page 109.

Push the pennies aside, saying:

"You may use any number you like so long as you have one more in the top row."

Turn your back while he sets up his rows.

Say, "Now name a number that's smaller than the number of pennies you have in the top row."

Suppose he says, "Five."

Say, "Remove that many pennies from the top row." Pause.

"Don't tell me the number of anything, but do you see the number of pennies left in the top row?"

Of course he does.

"Take that same number from the bottom row."

Then say: "I'm trying to concentrate now, but it's just too difficult. Too many pennies. Would you remove the rest of the pennies from the top row?"

Ask the spectator to concentrate on the number of pennies remaining. Finally, you say:

"I see . . . remaining in front of you . . . four pennies!"

You are right.

The trick is automatic. All you do is name one number lower than the number he announced. At the beginning, he said he was taking five pennies from the top row, so at the end of the trick, you came up with "four."

You will want to work it out for yourself, but here's an example:

The spectator lays out two rows; the top row is nine and the bottom row is eight.

```
1  2  3  4  5  6  7  8  9
1  2  3  4  5  6  7  8
```

He takes six pennies from the top row.

<pre>
1   2   3
1   2   3   4   5   6   7   8
</pre>

He notes how many are left in the top row and takes that many from the bottom row.

<pre>
1   2   3
1   2   3   4   5
</pre>

He removes the top row. And you have five left, one less than the number originally removed from the top row.

Naturally, the trick shouldn't be repeated. But you can follow up with the very similar *Give and Take*, immediately following.

Give and Take

You could perform the preceding trick and then do this one. Together they convincingly establish your telepathic powers. This one can, and probably should, be repeated at least once.

You're going to try another experiment in telepathy. Turn your back. This time your assistant is to make two rows of coins, with the *same number* in each row.

Say to your assistant:

"You may add coins or remove coins from either row, using additional coins or discarding coins. You may move coins from one row to the other. But you must tell me exactly what you're doing each time. For instance, if you're putting two more coins into the top row, you must tell me that. If you're transferring three coins from the top row to the bottom row, you must tell me that. And so on."

Here's the secret: As your assistant tells you of his various moves, you follow along mentally, *assuming* that he has seven coins in each row to start with, although you could actually use any number of coins. So at the beginning, say to yourself, "Seven, seven."

Your assistant says, "I removed three from the top row."

Say to yourself, "Four, seven."

There are now four coins in the top row, and seven in the bottom row.

Your assistant says, "I'm transferring two from the top row to the bottom row."

Say to yourself, "Two, nine."

Your helper says:

"I'm adding four to the top row."

Say to yourself, "Six, nine."

Assume that the spectator is done making his moves.

There are more coins on the bottom than on the top, so you say:

"Count the coins on top. Take that number away from the bottom."

This will leave three on the bottom.

"Now please take away the top row."

Concentrate and then announce that the number left is three.

Once more, all you need to do is follow the spectator's moves with your model of two rows of seven coins each.

Suppose that the spectator started with two rows of eleven coins each. He takes three from the top.

1	2	3	4	5	6	7	8			
1	2	3	4	5	6	7	8	9	10	11

He transfers two coins from the top row to the bottom row.

```
1  2  3  4  5  6
1  2  3  4  5  6  7  8  9  10  11  12  13
```

He adds four coins to the top row.

```
1  2  3  4  5  6  7  8  9  10
1  2  3  4  5  6  7  8  9  10  11  12  13
```

You direct the spectator to count the number of coins in the top row and remove that many from the bottom row.

```
1  2  3  4  5  6  7  8  9  10
1  2  3
```

Now he is to remove the top row. The result is three, just as it would have been if he had started with two rows of seven or *any* two rows of coins, so long as they were the same number.

To sum up, follow the spectator's moves, using your model of two rows of seven coins each. When the spectator is done, have him count the shorter row (you will refer to it as the top or bottom row) and remove that number of pennies from the other row. You then have him remove the original shorter row (again, refer to it as the top or bottom row).

If the spectator is making moves so swiftly that you can't keep up, tell him:

"Please slow down. It's very difficult trying to concentrate when you go so fast."

Clockwork

This coin trick is based on an old card trick. In the card trick, the magician seems to declare the number of red and black cards in two piles. In this coin trick, the magician seems to know how many heads and tails are in two groups of coins.

You need twelve coins of the same type. Use quarters because they show up well. You'll also need one odd coin to use as a marker; use a penny because it is strikingly different from the quarters.

Ask the spectator to assist you. Then lay out the quarters in the form of a clock, all of them head side up. Explain, "This is a clock, and this penny marks the quarter that is at 12 o'clock." Place the penny above the quarter (from the spectator's view). Illus. 77 shows what the spectator sees as he looks at the quarters.

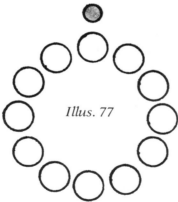

Illus. 77

Turn away, saying:
"Would you please turn over two of the quarters."
Pause, and say:
"Now turn over four other quarters."
Actually, you could simply say:
"Please turn over six of the quarters."

But the other method helps disguise the principle.

Then direct the spectator to turn over the quarters at two o'clock, four o'clock, six o'clock, eight o'clock, ten o'clock, and twelve o'clock. Naturally, give him time to turn over the appropriate coins.

Ask the spectator to slide to one side the quarters at one o'clock, three o'clock, five o'clock, seven o'clock, nine o'clock, and eleven o'clock. Tell the spectator:

"You now have two separate groups of coins. If I have correctly guided your moves, you should have the same number of heads and tails in each group."

Turn around and help the spectator verify that this is so.

You may repeat the trick, varying it somewhat. Again lay out the quarters head side up and mark twelve o'clock with the penny. Turn away. This time have the spectator turn over one coin, then two other coins, and finally three other coins—again, six in all.

Give these directions, leaving time for the spectator to perform the moves:

"Turn over the quarter at one o'clock. Turn over the one at two o'clock. Slide to one side the quarter at three o'clock. Turn over the quarter at four o'clock. Slide away the one at five o'clock. Turn over the quarter at six. Slide away the one at seven. Slide away the one at eight. And slide away the one at nine. Turn over the one at ten. Turn over the one at eleven. And slide away the one at twelve o'clock."

Again, you explain that if you have arranged things properly, both piles should now have the same number of heads and tails.

What you've done is precisely the same thing you did the first time. You have had the spectator turn over six coins and slide away the six other coins.

You need not follow the order given above. As a matter of fact, always make it different. Start at one o'clock and work around the clock to twelve. As you go, use your fingers to keep track of the number you've had the spectator turn over. When you hit finger number six, have him slide the rest aside.

Do you see why this trick works? Don't feel sheepish if you don't; the secret is quite subtle.

Put twelve coins in front of you in a group, face side up. Turn over any six. You have six heads and six tails. Now separate the coins into any two groups of six. Look at group one. Suppose you see two heads and four tails. In group two you will see two tails and four heads—the exact opposite. Obviously, if you turn over all the coins in one group, the two groups will match. This is precisely what happens with this trick.

Slide the two groups together. You have six heads and six tails. Randomly separate the coins into two groups of six. Examine the two groups. It is *inevitable* that you will have the same number of heads in one group as you have tails in the other, and vice versa. Turn over all the coins in one group, and the groups will match.

Play with this principle. You may end up with an even better trick.

Your Choice _____

In this trick you'll correctly predict which of four coins a spectator will choose.

Ask a spectator to assist you. In a row on the table, place a penny, nickel, dime, and quarter. The coins should be about 3″ apart. The dime should be the second coin from the spectator's right.

Unknown to your audience, you're holding a dime in a loose fist in your left hand.

Ask the spectator to place his hand on one of the coins. If he is right-handed, chances are strong that he will cover the dime, the second coin from his right. Suppose he covers the dime. Indicate with your right hand that he is to move his hand off the coin. Pick the coin up in your right hand. Hold each hand in front of you in knuckles-up fists. Slowly open your hands, showing that you have a dime in each. Smile, saying, "I was right."

If he covers a different coin, say:

"And one with the other hand."

Suppose he covers the dime with the other hand. With your right hand, pick up the uncovered coins and set them aside.

Say, "Hand me one, please."

If he hands you the dime, take it in your right hand and complete the trick as before, saying, "I was right."

If he hands you the other coin, take it in your right hand and set it aside with the others. Point to the dime on the table with your right first finger. Then point to your left hand and slowly open it, showing the dime.

Say, "I was right."

Suppose that the spectator covers a different coin with one hand and another different coin with the other hand. Gesture with your right hand that he is to hand you the coins he's covering. When he does, set them aside. Point to the remaining two coins, saying, "Hand me one, please." Proceed as you did in the paragraphs above by pointing.

Run through this trick several times, trying out the various options. It's really quite simple. It's important that you proceed without pause. Most of the time you won't have to bother with the patter: At the beginning the spectator will cover the dime.

Cover-Up _____

You should start with quite a few pennies on the table.

You're going to separate seven pennies, each with a different date, and you will set aside one penny with a date which matches that of one of the seven pennies.

As you go through the pennies, checking the dates, you might say:

"I need several pennies for this experiment. It's very difficult making choices."

Continue in this vein until you have the seven pennies spread out in the middle of the table. Push all the extra pennies aside. Hold up the penny which matches the date of one of the seven.

"This penny is most important. Can I get someone to hold his hand on top of this?"

Set that last penny to one side on the table, date side down, and get a spectator to cover the penny with his hand.

Make sure all seven pennies are date side down.

Get a volunteer to help you. Tell him this:

"We will take turns eliminating the pennies until only one is left. First, I'll cover two pennies with my hands. You choose either hand. We will eliminate the coin under it. Then you cover two pennies, and I'll choose one to eliminate. We'll keep this up until only one penny remains."

You follow this procedure, eliminating all the pennies but one. As each penny is eliminated, you push it to one side. Make sure the eliminated pennies are in a group of their own so that they can be checked later.

At the end, only one penny remains.

Say: "Now let's check the penny I set aside."

Ask the spectator who's holding the penny under his hand to read aloud the date on it. Have your volunteer read the date on the remaining penny. They match, and when the other six pennies are checked, their dates are found to be different.

To accomplish this wonderful result, all you must do is keep track of the penny which matches the one under the spectator's hand. You start the elimination by covering two coins other than the matching one. The spectator covers two coins; if he should cover the matching coin, choose the other hand. Again you cover two coins other than the matching one. And when the spectator covers two coins, you make sure that you don't choose the matching penny. Continue until only one penny is left. Naturally, it is the matching one.

After revealing that the two coins match, you can create a "sucker" ending by feigning reluctance to display the other six pennies. You might gesture towards the coins and say:

"These are unimportant, so we might as well put them with the others."

Probably someone will want to examine them, so you reluctantly give in. If no one says anything, say:

"Oh, well, you might as well check the dates."

Some in the audience may be actually disappointed that the dates are all different, but most will be amused.

Money Talks _____

Although the explanation of this trick may make it seem complicated, actually it isn't. In fact, it's a wonderful teaser which you will be called on to do again and again. The patter is quite important, so some suggestions are offered as the trick is described.

Get a spectator to assist you. Place three pennies and a quarter in a row on the table. Say to your assistant:

"You've undoubtedly heard the expression 'Money talks.' If that's true, a penny would speak in a whisper, and a quarter would be somewhat louder, and I'll try to *hear* that quarter."

Point to the coins.

"I'm going to turn my back. When I tell you to switch the coins, switch the quarter with the penny on either side of it."

Demonstrate a few movements, bringing the quarter to an end position.

"Of course if the quarter is on the end, you must switch it with the penny next to it."

Demonstrate.

"Now arrange the row any way you want, placing the quarter in any position among the three pennies."

When the spectator finishes rearranging the coins, you must casually note the position of the quarter. Suppose the spectator arranges the coins as follows, *from your point of view:*

O   O   O   O

To clarify, the quarter is second from his left and third from your left. Here's how you mentally catalogue the row of coins:

O   O   O   O
R   L   R   L

"R" stands for Right, and "L" stands for Left. In our example, the quarter is at "R," so all you need to remember is *Right*. The explanation will follow below.

Turn your back, and say, "Switch."

Have the spectator perform *five* switches in a row; then you'll provide further instructions. Pause between switches, and pretend to concentrate. Murmur things like:

"I'm not quite sure. Let's try another switch."

"It's not speaking to me yet. Switch once more."

"Concentrate on the quarter. Maybe one more switch."

"I'm starting to hear it. Switch again."

The idea, of course, is to distract the spectator from the *number* of switches made, which must be exactly five. Keep track of the switches made using your fingers.

After your helper has made five switches, say:

"Obviously, I have no way of knowing where the quarter is. But if you concentrate on it, perhaps it will speak to me."

Both of you concentrate a moment.

Say: "Now remove the coin on *your* right."

This is why you had to remember that the quarter was at the *Right* position.

Pause, and then say, "Make one more switch."

This last switch *always* places the quarter between the two remaining pennies.

Now he must remove the two outside coins. Say, "Take away the coin on the . . . right."

Concentrate a moment.

"Take away the coin on the left."

"If money talks," you say, "the coin remaining should be the quarter."

Turn around and look surprised when you see that the quarter is the remaining coin.

"It worked! Amazing."

This trick can be repeated a few times. If you plan to do it three times, vary the procedure the third time. When you come down to three coins, the quarter between two pennies, have the spectator pick up the middle coin. Pause a bit and say:

"Wait a minute! You just picked up *my* coin. The quarter just yelled that it's being smothered."

Turn around, saying, "I believe you're holding the quarter."

Here's why the trick works. Again, here are the possible positions of the quarter (as you look at them):

R   L   R   L

Suppose that the quarter is originally in one of the "R" positions. After five switches, the quarter will be in one of these two positions (as you look at them):

Tell the spectator to remove the coin at *his* right, and you're left with two possibilities:

After one more switch, the quarter is in the middle.

Essentially the same thing happens when the quarter starts in an "L" position. The only difference is that, after five switches, you tell the spectator to take away the coin on his left.

Mr. President _____

When this trick is properly performed, it appears to be real mind reading. To make this really work, however, the magician must convincingly act the role of the mentalist.

Place five coins on the table: a penny, a nickel, a dime, a quarter, and a fifty-cent piece.

Say, "Five of our most famous presidents are pictured on these coins."

Touch each as you say, "Lincoln, Jefferson, Roosevelt, Washington, and Kennedy." In your presentation, do *not* use the first names of the presidents; you'll see why later.

Get a volunteer and say to him:

"While I turn my back, I would like you to pick up one of these coins. Please hold the coin tightly in your hand, and hold your hand to your forehead as you concentrate on the president you have selected . . . Lincoln, Jefferson, Roosevelt, Washington, Kennedy."

Turn your back.

You're about to perform a subtle elimination procedure. To do so, you must remember N-O-I-O. These are the letters you will name, in order.

Say, "Are you concentrating on the president? I'm getting the letter 'N.' Is the letter 'N' in the president's name?"

If the spectator says yes, you continue. If he says no, say:

"Yes, it's the letter 'N.' It's in the first name. In fact, it's doubled in the first name. Franklin. You're thinking of Franklin Roosevelt!"

The spectator has said yes, so you say:

"The letter 'O' . . . I'm getting the letter 'O.' Is that right?"

If he says yes, continue. If he says no, say:

"The first name. I see the letter 'O' in the first name. John. It's John Kennedy!"

The spectator has said yes, so you say:

"I see an 'I.' Are you visualizing an 'I'?"

If he says yes, continue. If he says no, say:

"No, no, not the letter 'I.' The eye of a president whose picture is facing to the right. I see the picture of . . . President Thomas Jefferson!"

The spectator has said yes, so you concentrate a moment and say:

"I'm not getting the name. Please concentrate on the first name only. I'm getting the letter . . . 'O.' Is that right?

If he says yes, say:

"The president you're thinking of is . . . George Washington."

If he says no, say:

"Oh, that's my fault! I was visualizing a nickname ... Honest Abe. I was getting the 'O' in the word 'Honest.' You're thinking of Abraham Lincoln."

Act this one out with pauses, gradual discoveries, intense concentration—you'll have a little miracle.

When doing the first elimination, be sure to use this exact phrase or its equivalent:

"Is the letter 'N' in the president's name?"

If this isn't made clear, a spectator may assume that you are talking about the initial letter of the name.

This may be the only version of this trick which uses all five United States coins.

· 10 ·

ROUTINES

Clearly, the performance of particular coin tricks in a routine depends upon the circumstances. At a party, you would choose one kind of trick; seated at a table, another. Nevertheless, you should probably choose at least four tricks to use for *any* situation. The following four are entertaining and easy to perform:

Easy Vanish (page 13) with *Cough It Up* (page 27)

Quick Transpo (page 40)

Up One Sleeve and Down the Other (page 25)

Slap Through the Leg (page 23) with *Thumb-Palm Vanish* (page 15)

These four can be performed under any condition. If you're seated at a table, simply stand up and step back a little. Performing these four tricks takes about one minute. Usually your audience is ready for more, but if you have any doubts, quit. Don't bore people on purpose. Most often, people ask for more.

Have at least two additional routines ready: one for the table and one you can do standing up.

The following varied routines can be done at the table:

Leaping Pennies (page 52)

Too Many Pennies (page 97)

A Western Tale (page 99)

Through the Table (page 56)

Under the Table (page 57)

Row, Row (page 109) and *Give and Take* (page 111)
Mr. President (page 123)

You'll notice that some of the tricks depend upon a bit of sleight of hand, while others require no sleight.

The following routines can be done standing up:

Seven Cents (page 39)
Behind the Knee (page 29)
Your Choice (page 116)
Money Talks (page 120)
Hanky-Panky (page 69)
Not a Knot (page 75)
Vanish into Thin Air (page 31)

Your Choice and *Money Talks* both require a surface to place the coins on. You may use a regular table, an end table, or even the carpet.

Vanish into Thin Air is an excellent way to end a routine. The coin has disappeared altogether.

Children enjoy coin tricks. Any time you perform for children, you should include (besides your opening four) amusing tricks, such as the following:

Seven Cents (page 39)
A Western Tale (page 99)
Using Your Head (page 85)
Heads Up (page 87)
Stuck with a Penny (page 90)
S-T-R-E-T-C-H (page 80)
Silly! (page 81)

Avoid any tricks in which the children must move coins around or follow directions.

How do you develop a routine of your own? First go through all the tricks and pick out the ones you especially like and practise them. Test them in front of friends and relatives. If you don't have confidence in a particular trick, it's unlikely that you'll perform it well.

Mastery Levels Chart & Index

		Difficulty		
Coin Trick	**Page**	Easy	Harder	Advanced
Back of My Hand	47			★
Basic Vanish	17		★	
Basic Vanish (Variation)	20		★	
Behind the Knee	29			★
Bill Fold	41			★
Catch as Catch Can	28		★	
Classic Coins Through the Table	65			★
Clink!	35			★
Clockwork	114			★
Coins and Cards	59			★
Combined Vanish	20	★		
Cover-Up	118	★		
Cough It Up	27		★	
Cross-Up	49		★	
Easy Vanish	13	★		
Easy Call	89			★
Farmer's Will	95	★		
Flip-Flop	91			★
From a Spectator's Ear	23	★		
French Drop	9	★		
French Drop for One	12	★		
Give and Take	111		★	
Hand to Hand	51			★
Hanky-Panky	69		★	
Heads or Tails (1)	105		★	
Heads or Tails (2)	108		★	
Heads Up	87			★
Leaping Pennies	52		★	